Shorty
An Aviation Pioneer

The Story of Victor John Hatton

by
James Glassco Henderson

Front Cover Painting
Up to Knob Lake
by
Geoff Bennet

This painting, Acrylic on Masonite, 24" x 30" won first prize at the Canadian Aviation Artist's Association Annual Convention in September, 2000, and is used with the permission of the artist
It depicts Shorty Hatton flying the Burnelli "Flying Wing" CBY-3 to Knob Lake, Labrador for trials on 13 March, 1947.

The Artist
Geoff Bennet is a retired Royal Canadian Air Force officer who lives in Bridgewater, Nova Scotia

© Copyright 2004 James Glassco Henderson.
All rights reserved.

No part of this publication may be reproduced, stored in a retrieval system, or transmitted, in any form or by any means, electronic, mechanical, photocopying, recording, or otherwise, without the written prior permission of the author.

Note for Librarians: A cataloguing record for this book that includes the U.S. Library of Congress Classification number, the Library of Congress Call number and the Dewey Decimal cataloguing code is available from the Library and Archives of Canada. The complete cataloguing record can be obtained from the National Library's online database at: www.collectionscanada.ca/amicus/index-e.html
ISBN 1-4120-3897-9

Printed in Victoria, BC, Canada

TRAFFORD

This book was published *on-demand* in cooperation with Trafford Publishing.
On-demand publishing is a unique process and service of making a book available for retail sale to the public taking advantage of on-demand manufacturing and Internet marketing. **On-demand publishing** includes promotions, retail sales, manufacturing, order fulfilment, accounting and collecting royalties on behalf of the author.

Suite 6E, 2333 Government St.,
Victoria, B.C. V8T 4P4, CANADA
Phone   250-383-6864
Toll-free   1-888-232-4444
Fax   250-383-6804
E-mail   sales@trafford.com
www.trafford.com/robots/04-1705.html

10   9   8   7   6   5   4   3   2   1

CONTENTS

The Young Soldier	1
An Officer and a Gentleman	9
Life in the RCAF	19
Civilian Pilot	23
Maritime Mail	35
Night Mail	45
North Shore Mail	57
Bush Pilot	67
The National Airline	77
The End of an Era	81
Flying Salesman	87
Test Pilot	97
Hurricanes, Goblins and Helldivers	103
Flying Wing	113
Cold War	123
APPENDICES	
A The Silver Cigarette Box	131
B Shorty's Aircraft in Museum	135
C Notes on Sources	137
INDEX	142

PREFACE

When I was very little in the early 1930s my Henderson grandparents lived part way up the Hamilton, Ontario "mountain". Sometimes I went to stay with them and just before going to bed would sit on my Grannie's lap and look out over the city, at "Shorty's Light". It was on top of the Piggott building, Hamilton's only skyscraper with perhaps a dozen storeys. A flashing light that rotated a couple of times a minute, I knew it was there to guide my Uncle Shorty who was flying the night mail.

He was quite a man, living a life full of adventures. I never knew how many until, well into my sixties, I was given a chance to read his pilot's log books. Subsequent chats, with some of his contemporaries - Babe Woollett, Ken Molson and Peggy (Graham) Scully - convinced me that I should write his story. Mrs. Scully asked me if I knew about her early adventures when she had "lived in sin", and asked if I intended to include them. When I was a bit hesitant she said, "Oh you must - you can't sell a book without the naughty bits!"

Many wonderful hours spent with his widow and now the matriarch of our family, Gwen, led to more research. Aided by the late Tim Wight, a former colleague and broadcaster, who searched the Fort William archives at Thunder Bay and by Shorty's grandson, Nathan Mallett, who did some digging in the Hamilton area, I was able to produce a volume for family reading, in the late 1990s.

The advent of "on demand" publishing by the people at Trafford and the availability of many relevant photographs convinced me to publish the book for distribution beyond our immediate family. I am indebted to the staff of the National Aviation Museum for their help in obtaining photos from the Museum collection.

I have also included some bits of information that were familiar to those of us who lived through much of the twentieth century but which may not be known to Shorty's grandchildren or great grandchildren, for whom this book has been written.

J.G.H.
Barrie, Ontario
July 2004

For
Gwendolyn Sterling Hatton,
our beloved "Gongie",
who lived many of the adventures described in this book

INTRODUCTION

The bright blue June sky was reflected in the huge lake that seemed to stretch forever, like an ocean, outside the left window of the tiny aeroplane as it droned along, hugging the shore line. At times the land beneath hardly seemed to move at all as the single 200 horsepower engine fought the strong prevailing westerly winds which buffeted the small machine and made it difficult for the pilot to handle the metal cup half full of tea, poured, with some spillage, from the large thermos tucked behind the seat. He glanced at his watch and confirmed his suspicions that, with Kingston just behind him, the flight from Montreal was taking longer than he had calculated. Still there was no cause for concern. Even though it would take more than four hours to deliver the mail in the bags tucked in the cabin behind him to the Canadian Express Airport in the north part of Toronto it would still be much faster than the train.

The man at the controls was happy, never happier than in the cockpit and his concerns about future employment seemed to be behind him. At the age of 30 he had been through a war, a severe period of unemployment and a career as a military pilot during which he had survived a major crash. Now his fortunes had taken a turn for the better. He could not completely envision the future in this strange, large country which was just beginning to be opened up by civil aviation but he knew that it would be exciting. On the 15th of June, 1929, Shorty Hatton was at peace with the world.

The Young Soldier

At Christmas dinner in 1990 the grandchildren, young adults all, had dominated the conversation with speculation of war in the Persian Gulf. The meal had reached the point when most leaned back in their chairs while one or two cleared the table to make way for plum pudding and mincemeat pie when the Grandfather spoke. He had been silent until then and even now he spoke slowly in the deep voice, educated English accent and with the slight hesitation that was so familiar to all of them.

" I was just thinking back ..... it was 72 years last night that I was going up into the line from Reserve in Belgium...... and plodding through mud ....and how the devil the guides knew where to lead the various sections ...... there was nothing growing above two inches ..... nothing growing anywhere ..... a sea of mud. God knows how they knew where to go."

"A sea of mud "
Ypres Salient 1917

Silence fell over the room. Even the clatter of dishes from the adjoining kitchen stopped as he continued, "I finally got my section into where it was supposed to be ...... and we were in a big crater ..... about the size of this room I suppose...... if you got down too far you'd be in the water .... you had between three and four feet from the surface of the mud to the water ....it was all right in the dark because nobody could see you but if you popped your head up in the daylight you'd be in sight of the Huns ....during the night the shells would be coming over and they would go down through the mud until they hit the rock bottom ....and they would explode the detonator and whoosh ....up went the column of liquid mud ....and for at least twenty seconds it would be like a bath tap being turned on into a full tub of water.........that was the mud coming back ..... and in the morning you'd look around in this shell hole we were in ....it was very nice - - - there was a broken bedstead and three dead Huns floating in the water. That was Christmas morning."

On that 1917 Christmas morning the Grandfather had been known formally as 305563 Lance Corporal Hatton, Victor John, The London Rifle Brigade, British Expeditionary Force but, in spite of the fact that he was not unusually small, his friends called him Shorty. Although he was yet to celebrate his 19th birthday he was already an experienced veteran. He had joined the British Army in April that year the moment he reached the age of 18 and six months later had been sent with his unit to the continent to become part of the British Expeditionary Force deployed in the Ypres area.

> **"my section"**
> As a lance-corporal, Shorty was in charge of a section of 8 or 10 men. There were four sections in a platoon which was commanded by a lieutenant. Four platoons together made a company which was commanded by a major. Shorty's battalion, the 5th London Rifles, was composed of four companies and was commanded by a lieutenant-colonel.

Ypres is a small town in the Flanders region of Belgium, not far from the French border. During the devastating German attacks early in the First World War, the advancing enemy had halted briefly to regroup within rifle shot range of it. In the spring of 1915, in an attack all across the line, the Germans moved forward everywhere, except in the immediate area of Ypres. There, in spite of being inundated with poison gas in its first use as a military weapon, the Canadians held the line and a salient was formed with the German Army on three sides. The salient was almost, but not quite, untenable. It was completely dominated by the Germans who could see and shoot at everything in it. The sensible move would have been to withdraw and let the Germans have these few yards of tactically insignificant ground, but military leadership in the First World War was not characterized by common sense. One British general proposed just such a move and was promptly relieved of his command. For nearly three years the Ypres salient continued to exist and became, arguably, the filthiest area in the filthiest war in history. It has been estimated that of the million men who died in the war, fully one quarter of them lost their lives around Ypres.

In the summer of 1917 the Allied commanders decided to attack through it and on the 31st of July, the men of the British 5th Army climbed out of their trenches and, in what the history books call the Third Battle of Ypres, started to cross the muddy ground that lay between them and the enemy. 156 days and 250 thousand casualties later, in November, with the salient expanded enough to include the devastated village of Passchendaele, the battle formally ended. Ninety thousand of those casualties were listed as missing in the mud where they simply disappeared. Many had been buried as unknown soldiers but the bodies of 42 thousand of them were never found.

Shorty had been born in Plymouth, England, the second of Sarah and Joseph Monk Hatton's two sons, on April 13th, 1899. He was educated at Liskeard County School and the Plymouth Grammar School where his teachers, no doubt, recognized a neat orderly mind that approached all problems with meticulous care and logic, coupled with the zeal and keenness which characterized his approach to life and which prompted him to go to war at the earliest possible moment. On leaving school he had joined the family firm, Messrs J & R Monk (Wholesale Textile) where he was employed in the "Counting House ", i.e, the accounts department. There he learned the rudiments of bookkeeping and further developed his logical mind and penchant for crossing all the t's and dotting all the i's.

Plymouth

Plymouth is a seaport and naval base in Cornwall in Southern England. Drake played his famous game of bowls there before setting sail to defeat the Spanish Armada in 1588. In 1620 the Pilgrims sailed from Plymouth for the New World. During the Second World War (1939-45) the city centre was heavily damaged in German air raids, but in Shorty's time, it looked like this photograph.

Liskeard, where he first went to school, is a small town a few miles to the north west of Plymouth

The First World War started in August 1914, when he was only fifteen years old and still in school. His brother Bill, four years older, had gone into military service and, like so many young men of the era he had waited impatiently until he was old enough to take his own place in the ranks.

It is safe to say that he had no concept of the misery of life in the trenches when he volunteered. It is one of the great tragedies of the First World War that only those who were actually in the trenches had any idea of the conditions. It was almost as though there was a great conspiracy on the part of the soldiers to protect the innocence of those at home. Very few letters ever spoke of the appalling conditions. The newspapers talked incessantly of glory and gallantry, never of the filth and misery. Even the senior military commanders, who frequently established their headquarters in luxurious chateaux in the rear areas, appeared to have little knowledge of the conditions in which those under their command existed.

Shorty, like so many other young men of his day, was sheltered from the truth until he was forced to endure it, but once immersed in it he persevered. It was not until years later that he mentioned it, "People talk about disgusting things - I don't think anything could equal the Ypres salient in those days. It was hell."

His first taste of battle had come on the 22nd of November when the London Rifle Brigade as part of XVII Corps attacked the German defensive positions in the Hindenberg Line in one of the last gasps of the Third Battle of Ypres. The battalion succeeded in capturing its objective, a small wood called "Tadpole Copse", vital ground in the area of Moeuvre. They hung on to the feature in spite of repeated German counter attacks which included, on the 30th, a concentrated gas attack which decimated battalion headquarters. It left an impression on the young soldier that he never forgot.

"Chlorine, which was poison gas and rather nasty was green. Then there was Mustard gas which was known as yellow cross gas. Then there was the blue cross gas which was Phosgene which was a very, very dangerous thing. About three puffs of this and you'd had it. But the mustard gas would poison everything around you. A shell hole full of water and if you wanted to use it for washing - you'd never dare drink it - but even for washing the mustard gas would affect you and you'd come out with ghastly blisters. Even if you stepped in it, it would be the same thing."

Of course the men were equipped with gas masks but wearing them was not pleasant. "If you had to sit for eight hours with a gas mask on its not very comfortable".

And there was always the danger of being wounded in a gas attack. "If a man got hit, as soon as he was wounded he'd be gasping - the first thing he would want, just to get the damned thing off and he'd be immediately gassed on top of the wound."

On December 2nd, the battalion was relieved and went into reserve until Christmas Eve. Having enjoyed their Christmas dinner on the 23rd, they moved forward into the misery that Shorty was to describe so many years later.

At the end of January he was transferred to a sister unit, the 28th London Regiment (The Artist's Rifles), which had suffered heavy casualties earlier in the month. It was a most unusual battalion having been formed initially in the 1870's by a group of London artists - painters, writers and sculptors who wanted to provide service to the nation in a militia type organization. At the start of the war the Regiment had imposed such high standards on those trying to join that it had difficulty getting into action. Although it had moved into France very early in the war it was held as a reserve unit from which its men were drawn for officer training. Junior officers were dying at an alarming rate throughout the British Expeditionary Force and the soldiers of the Artist's Rifles, with their high standards of education and fitness, were ideally suited for officer training. That standard was maintained over the years and following service in the Second World War the regiment became the basis of Britain's elite Special Air Service.

In January 1918, when Shorty joined they were in the Ypres salient and, as he later explained, spent the rest of the bitterly cold winter moving in and out of the line, "You were there for 48 hours - you couldn't stay for more than 48 hours - you went back to the rear."

That miserable winter came to an end abruptly on March 21st, 1918 when the German Army attacked south of Ypres. By the 23rd The Artists Rifles were completely surrounded and in the bitter fighting one whole company, a quarter of the battalion, simply disappeared The rest fought their way to the rear and joined in the general British withdrawal. The Germans had considerable success driving a wedge between the British and French armies and it was feared that they would force the British back to the English Channel as they were to do so successfully a few years later in the early days of the Second World War. But the Allied armies held the line and managed to stop the enemy just 65 kilometres away from Paris.

By the end of July the German attacks petered out and the 18th of August found the British Army attacking on the Scarpe River as part of a huge Allied offensive. It succeeded and the Allies were, for the first time, able to drive the Germans farther and farther back until the memorable day, November 9th, when the Artists Rifles moved forward the unheard of distance of 8 miles. And then it all came to an end on the date we still mark on our calendars, November 11th.

It was a long time coming for Shorty and the others who had learned to endure the never ending mud, pain and terror. About the only comfort for the men

"You couldn't stay for more than 48 hours"
British troops in the trenches Ypres 1917

Imperial War Museum Photo

in the trenches was tobacco and while some of the older traditionalists stuck with their pipes many of the younger men, including Shorty, developed a taste for the newly invented cigarette. Arrangements had been made to order them at home from the factory and they became a popular form of gift for the boys at the front. One brand, Willis Wild Woodbine, was delivered for the cost of ten for a penny. There were other, more expensive brands, but cigarettes were cheap and Shorty, along with thousands of others developed the smoking habit.

With the end of hostilities the soldiers, naturally enough, wanted to go home as quickly as possible but there were still many problems to be solved and The British Expeditionary Force stayed on the continent for a long time after the armistice. The generals pointed out that it was only an armistice, not a peace treaty and that the Germans still seemed to have a lot of men under arms. Besides there were mines, unexploded shells and grenades all over the place to be cleaned up. As a relative newcomer to the service Shorty was not entitled to be among the first to go home. He continued to serve in The Artist's Rifles in Germany as a Warrant Officer 2nd Class (Company Sergeant Major) during a period when the army was rapidly returning to the spit and shine of peacetime soldiering. Perhaps it was during this time that he developed his habit of always being immaculately outfitted and clean shaven.

Over 1919 the army was reduced in size and eventually The Artists went home but Shorty stayed on as a Colour Sergeant (Company Quartermaster Sergeant) in the 17th London Regiment. The rank of Colour Sergeant, also known in some regiments as Staff Sergeant, is about half way up the ladder of non-commissioned ranks between sergeant and sergeant-major. Each rifle company of about 200 men would have one Colour Sergeant who operated the company stores. In this job (Company Quartermaster Sergeant) he was responsible for ensuring that all material available for the company was in good condition, securely stored and readily available when and where it was needed. It involved a limited degree of record keeping and made him the company logistician, the perfect job for a man who had displayed a penchant for meticulous attention to detail, coupled with accounting experience. During this period he was able to see something of the continent and managed to pick up enough of the French language to be able to converse in it with the locals, a skill that would be helpful in the years to come. Finally in October 1919, he went home to England and on November 13th he was demobilized and his name placed on the reserve army list.

Work was hard to come by. Britain continued to struggle financially and many young men who had fought in the war were faced with hard times. In his case the difficulties were exacerbated by family problems. His parents had separated and he was at odds with his father over the split. Bill had done what so many young Britons had done for generations and gone out into the Empire to seek his fortune. He was in Calcutta working for the Reilly Motor company. Given the limited opportunities, Shorty felt there was nothing to hold him in England and he followed his brother on the long sea voyage to India. He stayed for a while but nothing substantial materialized and the spring of 1921 found him back in England.

**Rank Badges
British Army Non-Commissioned Officeers
World War I**

The country he came home to was in not much better shape than the one he had left. About a million men were looking for work. One writer has described an unsuccessful search for work in London and finally spending the night, wrapped up in his military greatcoat, on a bench along the Thames embankment in the heart of the nation's capital. When he awoke he was astonished to find that he was not alone. Everywhere he looked - on the other benches, along the pavement and on the grass, were many many others, dressed as he was and all unemployed.

The situation was not helped by labour problems in the coal mines, upon which all other industries depended. The miners had called a strike in March of 1919, again in October of the same year and now in March, 1921 when the government failed to nationalize the coal mines as they had demanded, they went out again. The government prepared to declare a State of Emergency, but the Regular Army was overseas or in Ireland where there were other problems. It was decided to activate a number of reserve units in a Special Defence Force to be used if and when needed.

On April 13, 1921, his 22nd birthday, Shorty rejoined his old unit, the London Rifle Brigade of the SDF on a special 90 day enlistment. He was granted his former rank, Colour Sergeant, for employment as a Company Quartermaster Sergeant. At the end of the 90 day period his service was extended for a year to 25th of July 1922.

On that date he was accepted for a further year's army service but a few days later, on August 1st, 1922, he went before a Medical Board and the doctors found him " fit for flying duties as a pilot".

An Officer and a Gentleman

The citizens of the tiny village of Shotwick, Cheshire, just north of the River Dee in the west of England were accustomed to the buzz of aircraft from the RAF's # 5 Flying Training School just a few miles away at Sealand. They had even been aware that sometimes the flimsy Avro 504Ks of the school came down in their fields or the fields of their neighbours, but the crash on an early autumn Monday in 1922 was much worse than anything they had seen before. The tail, or at least parts of it, appeared to have come off in flight and the plane had fallen to the ground completely out of control. When they reached its remains they were appalled to find the battered bodies of two apparently dead aviators lying, still and unmoving, in the tangled wreckage.

The tail appeared to have come off in flight ....
From an original black and white wash painting by R.W.Bradford for the Avro News, 1952. With permission

Shorty was one of those aviators and, at first, no one even bothered to attempt first aid. He was covered with blood, his right arm and left leg were bent into unnatural angles, his face was battered and he showed no signs of life. But as the bodies were removed from the wreckage it became apparent that he, unlike his companion, still lived and he was rushed to the Infirmary at nearby Chester. There the doctors initially diagnosed his injuries as a broken right arm, smashed left knee and multiple injuries to the lower left side of his face. Later, as he lay in hospital, other injuries were discovered. His mother came to visit and care for him as best she could. One day she carefully peeled some grapes and gently attempted to slip them, one at a time into his wired mouth, only to be rebuffed with cries of intense pain. The doctors examined the interior of his mouth and discovered severe damage to his palate where a piece of metal had lodged itself. He was to stay in the infirmary for a month and a half and then moved to the RAF Hospital at Halton in Buckinghamshire where he spent the next six months recuperating.

Just a month before the crash, on September 2nd, he had been granted a Short Service Commission as a Pilot Officer on probation in the Royal Air Force and posted to 5 FTS for the pilot's course of instruction. This flight on October 9th, with an instructor at the controls, was one of his first.

All military organizations face a common problem with the biological fact that their members grow older and it is even more acute in the air forces of the world. They have learned that it takes a certain sort of individual, intelligent, usually well educated and physically fit with quick reactions to fly an aeroplane. Unfortunately the latter characteristic tends to fade in all of us as the years go by and this leaves the air force with a problem. What do you do with pilots whose natural physical skills start deteriorating with age? Having recruited the sort of people who could probably establish comfortable careers for themselves in almost any other line of work, the air force now finds itself in the position of not really wanting these aging thirty year olds any more. The answer is the short service commission by which pilots are engaged for a specific period of time and in the early 1920's the RAF's Short Service Commission was for a period of four years. As political priorities changed and the need for more or less warriors changed with them, there would be adjustments to the policy, but when Shorty transferred from the London Rifles of the British Army to the Royal Air Force it was to be for a four year period during which he would be taught to fly and then employed in some of the many tasks facing the defence establishment of the day.

The RAF had been formed on April 1st in the last year of the war by amalgamating the British Army's Royal Flying Corps with the Royal Naval Air

Service. When the war ended it was reduced from 188 to 33 squadrons but as Britain continued to manage its Empire the need for more was recognized. Aside from the very real problems close to home in Ireland, there were requirements for squadrons in Egypt, in the Mediterranean, Mesopotamia (Iraq), India and Germany, to say nothing of fighters, bombers and coastal patrol aircraft for the protection of the British Isles. In addition there was a need for training establishments including flying schools, schools for the highly skilled mechanics needed to maintain the aircraft, and colleges for the education and further development of officers.

When Shorty embarked on his air force career it was reasonable to expect that he would be flying on operations with one of those squadrons within a year but his accident delayed his training and he spent three quarters of that year recuperating from the crash at Shotwick. As his health improved so did his social life which was necessarily restricted by the need for him to stay in hospital. Nevertheless he met and courted an attractive young woman. While they saw a great deal of one another during his convalescence, his intentions were apparently more honourable than hers, because when he asked her to marry him she declined.

Finally, after all that time in hospital followed by a couple of weeks sick leave, he was once again declared

Avro 504K

The original Avro 504 was designed in 1913 by Sir Alliot Verdon-Roe. The aircraft had a top speed of 82 mph. (132 km/h), could climb to 10,000 feet in 19 minutes and could stay aloft for three hours. It could operate at the "extreme height" of 13,000 ft (3960 m). The 504K Trainer was introduced in 1917, and sported a new type of universal engine mount which consisted of two bearer plates that could accommodate any sort of engine. The 504K was variously fitted with the 100 hp Gnome B Monosoupape, the 110 hp Le Rhône 9J, and the 130 hp Clerget 9B engine.

A training advantage was the ease with which students and instructors could communicate in the cockpit, thanks to the "Gosport Speaking Tube". The 504's relatively light weight in comparison to its wing size prevented the plane from dropping dramatically when power was reduced, and the "forgiving" quality of its controls were ideal for training. So too was the skid that could be outfitted under the nose, designed to prevent tipping during landing.

Royal Air Force Photo

fit and on May 19th, 1923 returned to 5 FTS at Sealand to start his pilot training all over again. He never discussed the fear he must have felt on stepping back into an AVRO 504K for the first time, but in later years it was obvious that he was never very comfortable in an aeroplane when someone else was at the controls. When he was flying the machine it was a different story. He was a natural pilot, completely at home in the air. Years later his second daughter, Sue, was astonished when, in her teens, she realized for the first time the change that came over him when he was flying. He had taken her for a flight and she suddenly realized, as he settled in the cockpit, that he was a completely different person from the father she had always known at home. He was much more alive and she recalled this staid, very proper man did something he had never done before, "He winked at me!"

Many customs of the service, including the style of the uniforms, had been inherited from the Army and Navy and while some of them changed with usage and new values they were still part of the RAF officer's life long after the Second World War. Life as a commissioned officer, albeit one on probation, was very different from his previous military experience. In the British class system which still prevailed in the 1920s, officers were gentlemen, "officers by the grace of God and gentlemen by an Act of Parliament", while Other Ranks were not. In spite of his impeccable manners and gentle nature he had been, until the moment of commissioning, a member of Britain's lower classes in the eyes of the military and some other segments of society. Other Ranks were addressed by their last name, Officers by their rank. Other Ranks lived in barracks and ate in mess halls.

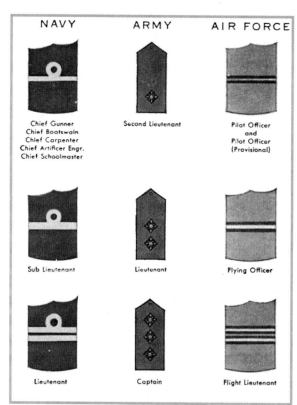

Junior Commissioned Ranks
British and Canadian Armed Forces
1920s - 1940s

The Mess System

The domestic arrangements for members of the British armed forces were similar in all three branches of the service and were based on the three tier rank structure. On the theory that it was bad for discipline for the various rank levels to mix socially, seperate facilities were maintained for commissioned and non-commissioned officers.

The privates and corporals were housed in barrack rooms and fed in mess halls. Canteens, where mild beer was available, were often provided in an effort to keep the troops out of unsavoury establishments that often sprang up outside the gates of the barracks.

Sergeants and Warrant Officers lived in seperate quarters and a Senior N.C.O.s mess where meals were served and rooms provided in which the members could meet, socialize and entertain.

Commissioned officers lived in the Officer's Mess which, typically, contained a dining room and several ante rooms (the equivalent of the living rooms, recreation rooms, libraries, etc. of well appointed private homes). While the Mess was provided by the government, many of the amenities in it were paid for by the members who were charged a regular subscription.

Officers had private bedrooms and dined in the Officer's Mess. Other Ranks were issued their uniforms of rough cloth which buttoned at the neck, Officers had theirs tailored, usually on Savile Row in London. They also had the services of a batman, a military valet who made sure that his officer was always immaculately dressed in the appropriate costume of the moment. This normally consisted of a tailored pale blue jacket with shirt and tie worn with riding breeches and shiny black knee high riding boots, the whole set off with a narrow malacca cane with which the young officer could slap his boots as though he was about to ride off to hunt foxes. It did not harm their careers if they frequently did hunt foxes or engage in other activities involving horses. Their social lives were centered around the Officer's Mess and they were expected to dress for dinner each evening. Frequently they got all dolled up in Mess Kit or black tie and entertained other gentlemen (never gentlewomen) at Guest Nights, i.e., formal dinners. Not all of the traditions of these formal dinners were fully appreciated by the younger officers and Shorty remembered one Padre who insisted on pronouncing a lengthy and convoluted Grace before dining. In his absence the Mess President was required to substitute for him and on one such occasion, the President arose from his chair, looked around the table and gave his version of the Blessing, "Padre here ? No ? Thank God".

The working uniform for flying duties was a white, one piece coverall in milder weather and the world famous Sidcot one piece flying suit (not unlike the suits worn by modern snowmobile enthusiasts) when it was cooler. A leather helmet had goggles and a mouth covering for the rubber Gosport Tube through which pilot and instructor could talk to one another. The white silk scarf made famous in countless movies about early aviation was not approved for use by student pilots.

The training was conducted in two-seater Avro 504Ks in which the instructor sat in the back where he could watch the student up front and , when necessary, take over from him. Training in the air consisted of the tried and true method of demonstration, followed by imitation and endless practice under the watchful eye of the instructor. Finally there was the magic moment when, judging that he had nothing more to teach, the instructor allowed the student to try it on his own. All of which was supplemented by classroom work in which the student was inundated with information about regulations and the theory of flight. The process has not changed appreciably since then.

His flying training continued until February 1924 when he was authorized to sew pilots wings on the left breast of his jacket just above the ribbons of the British War Medal and the Victory Medal which indicated his wartime service. He had achieved a grade of 81% on his elementary flying training and was considered "Suitable as Gunnery Instructor". His  probationary status was removed and he was promoted to the rank of Flying Officer. On March 14th, he was posted to No. 7 (Bomber) Squadron at Bircham Newton in Norfolk for training on twin engine aircraft.

7 Squadron had been formed the year before for the specific purpose of being equipped with twin engine machines and it had received a number of Vickers Vimy bombers.

Over the month of April 1924 he flew many hours in the Vimy and, at the end of the month was awarded a "Distinguished Pass" as he completed his twin engine instruction. Then, in a move all too typical of military organizations, he was promptly posted to a unit where his newly developed skill were not needed.

At the same RAF Station, Bircham Newton, another unit, No. 99 (Bomber) Squadron, was being activated to fly the newly built Avro 549 Aldershot biplane, the last of the RAF's big single engine bombers and Shorty joined it as one of its first pilots. The Aldershot, only served in the RAF for two years. For one of those years Shorty flew the machine, mostly on night flights.

During that same period he was required from time to time to fly other aircraft. In an economy measure some of the Flying Training Schools had been closed and students were sent to operational squadrons to complete their training. Along with them came the dual place Avro 504Ks which the experienced pilots managed to use, not always for official purposes. On one flight Shorty had taken a 504K to visit a young lady and having landed close to her home had to manufacture a reason for his "forced landing". In an early manifestation of his technical skills, which would be so important in years to come, he disabled the engine in such a way that it appeared as though there had been a plausible engine failure. Frequently there was no need to create reasons. The engines managed to fail regularly and the pilots became skilled at finding fields in which to set down. On one such occasion the local people, who were out shooting as he fluttered into their beet field, presented him with a freshly killed hare. The proud donor told him that she had watched him overhead just as she shot at it and swore to the others that if he landed she would give it to him.

Avro 549 Aldershot
Single Rolls Royce Condor 650 HP Engine
Max speed: 110 mph (177 KmH)
Ceiling: 14,500 ft (4,170 M)
Range: 650 miles (1,046 KM)
This heavy bomber was brought into service in the RAF briefly in 1922. It was designed for a crew of five: two pilots and a gunner in an open cockpit plus a radio operator and a bomb aimer in an enclosed cabin.
Photo courtesy Canada Aviation Museum

May, 1925 saw him on the move to Aldergrove, near Belfast in Northern Ireland. During World War II Aldergrove would become a British terminal for aircraft being ferried across the Atlantic but in 1925 it was the home of No. 502 Squadron, RAF. 502 was was formed on May 25th as a cadre unit of the Special Reserve and Shorty was one of its original members.

Northern Ireland had existed as an entity for only four years and was not quite a complete nation. The British Government of Ireland Act of 1920 had established a subordinate government for the largely protestant northern part of the island of Ireland. The remainder, with its largely Roman Catholic population, known in those days as The Irish Free State, eventually became a self-governing dominion with the same autonomy as Canada and Australia. Northern Ireland with its capital at Stormont, near Belfast, elected a parliament of its own with responsibility for local matters but others, including foreign affairs and the armed forces, continued to be controlled from London. This solution to the disagreements between the citizens of the island and the British government had only been reached after nasty fighting over a number of years and, as history was to prove, was not a particularly effective one. Throughout the 1920's both the Protestants and the Catholics expanded their underground armed elements and between 1920 and 1922 there were any number of riots in the streets of Belfast and many murders on both sides. The differences have never been resolved and over the years there have been varying degrees of violence short of declared war. The governments of Northern Ireland and the Irish Republic watched each other closely but, for a variety of reasons, neither openly opposed the other. Still there was constant underground simmering which must have concerned members of the Royal Air Force at Aldergrove in Antrim county. Even though it was in a largely protestant area, it was only a few miles west of Belfast where violence had been common and security measures were always a high priority. Shorty served there for two years.

Vickers Vimy
Two Rolls Royce Eagle VIII 360 hp engines
Max Speed 103 mph (165 kmh)
Ceiling: 7,000 feet (2000 M)
Range: 900 miles (1448 KM)

The Vimy was designed in World War One as a strategic bomber capable of attacking targets in Germany. It first flew on 30th November, 1917, and only token numbers arrived in France before the Armistice of 11th November, 1918. The Vimy is remembered for its pioneering flights, including the first non-stop east to west crossing of the Atlantic by Alcock and Brown in 1919, the first England to Australia flight of Ross and Keith Smith and crew; and the attempted first England to South Africa flight of van Rynevald and Brand.

Royal Air Force Photo

As a squadron of the Special Reserve, 502 was comprised mostly of reservists who served on a part time basis, getting flying in when they could take time off from their full time civilian jobs. They were supplemented by a small staff of regulars and as one of them, it was Shorty's job was to instruct the reserve pilots on flying the Vickers Vimy. Flying during the winter months was fairly limited, partly because of the weather and partly because the runways were not paved. While smaller aircraft did not damage the grass runways much, the heavier Vimys churned up the earth and when there had been heavy rain the machines were grounded by mud. Not all of the flying was directly related to training. There was a bit of show biz too. On one memorable occasion he was required to lead a V formation of three Vimys with little "fairy lights" strung all along the fuselage and around the wings and tail planes over the night time Military Tattoo in Belfast. His passenger was a flamboyant Irish theatrical personality who came dressed in purple trousers and equipped for the flight with a large green umbrella. They were to meet again years later in Canada when the passenger, Sir Tyrone Guthrie, was making a name for Stratford, Ontario by developing that city's Shakespearean Festival Theatre.

Now and then there was a chance to fly something new and shortly before Christmas in 1925, he was introduced to a new aircraft he would meet again over the years. The head of civil aviation, returning to London after a visit to Dublin, had landed to refuel his new DH 60 Moth before crossing the Irish Sea. The DH 60 was the first of a long line of Moths that would be built by de Havilland over the years and the prototype had made its first flight earlier that year. When a weather report convinced the civil servant that a flight across the sea at that time would not be wise, he departed by boat, leaving the pilot and aircraft at Aldergrove to wait out the weather. During his enforced visit with the RAF the pilot kindly offered some of the officers a flight in this new machine. Shorty was one of those who jumped at the opportunity and flew it - the third Moth ever built.

He also served as the unit Adjutant, a job he carried out "with success", according to his Commanding Officer. The Adjutant was the CO's personal staff officer with a special responsibility for the discipline of the junior officers. Traditionally he was required to be, "the epitome of dress and deportment". His superiors thought highly of Shorty's work and noted on his annual confidential report that he was "Extremely keen, reliable and sets a good example to his juniors. Trustworthy and painstaking." His flying skills were rated above average and he was graded "Excellent" under the heading "Zeal".

Since his four years service had started in September 1922 it was scheduled to end in 1926 but during his time at Aldergrove it was extended for a further year to 1927. While he may have wished to stay in the RAF even longer, the opportunity was not provided in spite of his good reports. At different times in its history, the RAF did convert Short Service Officers to Regular Commission status, but this was not one of them. In the late 1920's economy was on everyone's mind and the armed forces were scrambling to cut back without losing effectiveness. On September 2nd, 1927 he was, once again, transferred to the Reserve List, this time as a Flying Officer.

The situation was not much better than it had been in 1919, except that now he had new skills which he felt might be marketable. With several hundred hours in the air, many of them on twin engine machines, he was an accomplished aviator, qualified to fly most modern aircraft of the day. He had heard of the expansion of aviation in Canada, where wartime pilots had gone home to start small flying companies that were now opening up the areas of the country rarely seen by people of European stock. There was considerable contact between the RAF and the Royal Canadian Air Force. It had been formed on April 1st 1924 and the Canadians had obtained most of their aircraft from Britain. All of their senior officers had served in the RAF or its predecessors, the RNAS or RFC. It was common knowledge in RAF circles that the RCAF was charged with training pilots for the expanding civilian aviation industry and was looking for qualified instructors. It was also known that experienced pilots from Britain who were prepared to fly in the primitive conditions of the Canadian north were welcome in both military and civil aviation circles.

Shorty thought that sort of life might appeal to him and he made inquiries about it. In February, 1928 he underwent a medical examination for a civilian pilots licence and was declared fit by Air Ministry standards. Early in March he was able to upgrade his flying skill in a course at the RAF's Central Flying School at Upavon in Wiltshire on the Bristol fighter. On 9 March, 1928 he was issued British Air Ministry Pilot's Licence # 1307 and certified competent to fly the Bristol Advanced Training Biplane, Vickers Vimy Bomber, Avro 504K and Avro 504N. These latter two aircraft were in use in Canada as elementary flying training machines.

On April 1st, 1928 he formally resigned his commission in the Royal Air Force. On the same date, King George V issued a document " To our trusty and well beloved Victor John Hatton" that went on, "reposing especial Trust and Confidence in your Loyalty, Courage and good Conduct do by these Presents Constitute and Appoint you to be a Flying Officer in our Royal Canadian Air Force."

Life in the RCAF

The train from Toronto chugged into the railway station at Angus some 80 kilometres north of Toronto and the young man, fresh from England, stepped down to be met by a car and driver from nearby Camp Borden. It had been an eye opening trip for Shorty as it was to all those who moved to North America from "the Old Country". The wide open spaces, the long distances, the expanses of water and the countryside, even in well-settled Southern Quebec and Ontario were all very different from tiny, tidy England and bore no resemblance at all to his other overseas experiences on Continental Europe and in India. Everything, including the train, seemed to be much bigger. The car trundled along the dirt road through the village of Angus and along the winding paths cut through the trees to deposit him at the shack containing the headquarters of the Flying School. In the manner of all newly assigned officers in every military organization in the world, he reported to the Adjutant, was welcomed, assigned duties and taken to his living quarters. Flying Officer Victor John Hatton, Royal Canadian Air Force had arrived at his new station.

The air force that he joined on April 1st, 1928, while similar in outward appearances to the one he had just left, was quite different. The British force was a military organization created for and employed on tasks aimed at maintaining the vast British Empire. While the uniforms, regulations, customs and aircraft were the same as those of the RAF the Canadian force was orientated towards civilian flying and more than one author has described its pilots as "bush pilots in uniform".

The Royal Canadian Air Force had been formally created just four years before on 1 April 1924 after a shaky start at the end of the First World War. No one in Canada ever entertained the notion that it might actually be used for the defence of the nation and its aircraft and crews had been employed on such tasks as forest fire patrols, aerial photography and exploration, particularly in the far north. There was also a job that continued well beyond the end of the Second World War, the collection of ice movement information in the northern shipping lanes. But its main function, at the time Shorty joined, was the training of pilots and crews for civil flying operations. A job for which he, with over 900 hours hours at the controls of a variety of aircraft and his experience as a flying instructor in the RAF, was particularly suited.

At that time all flying training was conducted at Camp Borden. It had been established as a Royal Flying Corps training centre during the war and its extensive facilities, including hangars and other accommodation, were taken over by the Canadian Air Force in peacetime. Among other things inherited from the British were a number of AVRO 504s of various marks and some of them, very ancient by that time, were still in use for flying training.

Camp Borden
The Hangar line built originally for the Royal Flying Corps during World War I. Many of the hangers, which had been declared a National Historic Site, were still in use at the start of the 21st Century

Much of the flying training was conducted during the summer months when the weather was usually good and most of the students were Provisional Pilot Officers from the universities or the Royal Military College. This officer training scheme had been developed some years before and in it individuals could, over three successive summers, reach wings standard. For some there was a possibility of further Air Force service on graduation or an opportunity for employment in civil aviation. Similar plans existed in the Navy and Army and, in fact, the plan was reborn in the years following the Second World War when thousands of young university graduates found summer employment with reasonable financial remuneration and, at the end, a reserve commission in the forces. One of Shorty's pupils that summer was young Ernie McNab who, a few years later would, as a

Squadron Leader, command #1 Squadron, RCAF during the Battle of Britain and become the first RCAF pilot to shoot down an enemy aircraft in World War II.

On Parade at Camp Borden
This photo, taken in 1926 two years before Shorty joined the staff at the RCAF's #1 Service Flying Training School, shows the staff and students drawn up on parade for inspection. Note that most are wearing khaki summer uniforms but one officer is in winter blue. Officers (with canes, open collars and neckties) in front are wearing riding breeches one with rolled puttees the other in riding boots. The non-commissioned people are all in shorts with puttees. They include cadets under instruction who can be identified by the white band on their hats. These uniforms would have been unchanged in Shorty's time at Borden.
Photo Courtesy Canada Aviation Museum

Life at Borden was pleasant and, for the officers, centred around the mess. Individual officers were provided with a private bedroom, took their meals in a reasonably well appointed dining room and used the other mess rooms for reading, playing cards and billiards or just socializing around the bar. While the pay was not outstanding it was adequate and provided enough for an unmarried individual to meet his obligations in the mess and to have a bit left over to explore the neighbouring recreation areas and the growing city of Toronto a few miles to the south. Work for the instructional staff consisted mostly of flying with the summertime fledgling aviators and teaching them the skills they needed to have wings sewn on their tunics. Still it was a military organization and there was the inevitable paper work plus the occasional parade in which full uniform was required.

One such occasion took place in November, 1928 when Shorty joined five of his brother officers as pall bearers at the funeral of a fellow instructor, Flying Officer Arthur Edward Reynolds. He had been killed instantly when the moth he was flying on the afternoon of 1 November had crashed on the airfield at Borden moments after taking off. A passenger, one Major Currie from Ottawa, was severely injured. Full military honours were paid to Reynolds who, like Shorty, had joined the RCAF just months before after serving in the Royal Air Force. The funeral service was held at Trinity Anglican Church in Barrie. About fifty officers and non-commissioned officers formed the funeral cortege to the graveside at the Barrie Union Cemetery. The escort and firing party, under the unit adjutant, Flying Officer A.F Ingram, were followed by the gun carriage flanked by the pall bearers. Three rounds were fired over the grave by the firing party and a bugler played the last post.

Borden was the focal point of Canadian flying activity in those days and while there Shorty was able to make invaluable contacts with people in the business; people he would work with and who would become fast friends in the years to come. This was important because the RCAF, like its parent in Britain, had solved the problem of aging pilots by operating on a short service commission basis. Flying Officers were released from the service at 30; the age he would reach in April 1929, one year after joining the RCAF. During his year at Borden Shorty constantly had an eye out for his future in Canadian aviation and on January 4th, 1929 he was issued his first Canadian civilian pilot's licence, # 402.

One of the men he met at this time was R.O. "Bob" Denman of Hamilton, Ontario. As a teenager Bob Denman had served in the 2nd Canadian Battalion during the war and won the Distinguished Conduct Medal and the Military Medal. Upon being commissioned he had won his Royal Flying Corps pilot's wings and served in #148 Squadron of the Royal Air Force. The war ended for him in the summer of 1918 when his FE 2B bomber was shot down and he fractured his pelvis. Now he was involved with a group in Hamilton who had established a small airline, International Airways of Canada Limited. The company was on the lookout for qualified pilots and Denman maintained contacts with the RCAF, the major source of trained flyers. Even more valuable than recently trained youngsters were experienced pilots, such as Shorty, who had considerable experience in the air, and these Bob Denman courted openly with job offers.

Civilian Pilot

At 11:45 on the morning of Saturday, June 15th, 1929, a tiny high wing monoplane bearing the identifying letters G-CATU rolled along the runway at St Hubert airport south of Montreal, became airborne, turned west and climbed to two thousand feet. It fought strong headwinds along the St Lawrence River over Cornwall to Kingston then past Belleville edging along the north shore of Lake Ontario to land four hours and ten minutes later at the Canadian Air Express Airport in the north part of Toronto.

The plane was a Fairchild FC-2, it was loaded with mail and Shorty was the pilot. It was a typical flight, but not his first, for his new employer, International Airways of Hamilton. On June 4th he had particpated in an historic event when he flew one of two commemorative flights to mark the dedication of the new Kingston, Ontario airport. There were regular air mail flights between Montreal and Toronto but on this date the flight was broken at Kingston where the mail was specially marked. O.C Wallace had flown the first leg from Montreal to Kingston and Shorty the second leg from Kingston to Toronto.

Two days later he became involved in an event that he would not soon forget. Any modern aviator would have been appalled at the apparent madness of some thirty aircraft and two Goodyear blimps flipping in and out of a small airport as and when they chose with no radios and no air traffic control whatsoever. As Shorty later recalled with typical understatement, it was "rather hectic".

It was the gala opening of the Hamilton Airport on Sunday June 6th, 1929

> **Philately**
>
> Once countries started printing and selling postage stamps to pay for the delivery of mail, it was inevitable that people would start collecting them. Thus the great hobby/commercial enterprise known as philately was born. Postal authorities quickly realized that if people were prepared to pay for stamps they would be prepared to pay extra for specially marked stamped envelopes. From then on, special events, such as the first mail from one place to another were commemorated in special stamps and markings on the envelopes carrying those stamps. Envelopes were produced for the sole purpose of becoming souvenirs. They bear special cancellation marks and are known as "covers".
>
> With the introduction of air mail a new sub category of philately, aerophilately, developed. When new air mail routes were inaugurated, or other special aviation events took place, post offices routinely produced special stamps and suitably embellished, "first day covers" marked with a "cachet" (printed impression) describing the event. Occasionally such covers were also signed by the airmail pilot, although there is no evidence that Shorty ever did.

when the Steel City was showing the the world the newly built facility which local enthusiasts claimed was the most modern airport in the nation. An estimated six thousand people had travelled out to the field with its one hangar and two runways situated just north of Highway 8 between the city and Stoney Creek in an area that would, in later years be covered with suburban homes and shopping centres. The aircraft had come from a number of places and companies including Hamilton's own International Airways which was represented by four machines.

In those days at the end of the Roaring Twenties and just before the Great Depression, airline companies seemed to be forming, reforming and grouping at an alarming rate. J.V Elliot Limited begat Elliot Air Services which begat International Airways all in the space of a couple of years. Bob Denman was one of the principles in the creation of International and he had persuaded Shorty to join the company when his service in the RCAF ended.

Throughout the opening air show on that Sunday he was kept busy taking passengers for short rides in a company Fairchild but the highlight of the show was the air race. The Wentworth Air Derby was a race for aircraft of 85 horsepower or less over a 30 mile course. It was won by an International Airways pilot, Richard H. "Dick" Bibby, another former RAF pilot, flying a de Havilland Cirrus Moth, who covered the course from Caledonia to Hagersville in 22 minutes and 15 seconds. In addition to the race the show featured a few of Shorty's former colleagues in the Royal Canadian Air Force demonstrating Moths and the new Siskin fighters, the brass band of a local militia regiment, the Argyll and Sutherland Highlanders of Canada and, as a grand finale, a parachute jump by a Hamilton firefighter.

An event of some national historic significance took place at the show when Imperial Oil presented the President of the Aviation League of Canada, Major General J.H.MacBrien with a new de Havilland Gipsy Moth, CF-AAA, to be used by the League in its task of promoting aviation throughout the nation. General MacBrien and the gleaming white AAA with its bright red letters were to become a familiar sight at air shows across the country.

Civilian aircraft, even in those early flying days had to be registered with the Federal Government. International convention dictated identifying letters to individual nations for registration and initially, Canadian aircraft were registered as being in the British Empire and used the identifying letter G, followed by a C as the first of a four letter combination. Thus G-CATU could be easily identified as a Canadian machine. Starting on 1 January, 1929, Canadian aircraft were identified by a two letter group, CF, followed by a three letter group. CF-AAA was the

CF-AAA
Presented to Major General Mac Brien the founder of the Canadian Aviation League. This photo was taken on 1 June, 1933. The names of the places it had visited are printed on the side of the aircraft
Photo Courtesy the Canada Aviation Museum

**Major General James Howden MacBrien,
CV, CMG, DSO**
General MacBrien was born at Port Perry, ON on 30 June 1878. He served in the militia, the North-West Mounted Police and then the South African Constabulary 1901-06. A staff officer at the outbreak of WWI, he took command of the 12th Infantry Brigade in 1916 and later Chief of the General Staff, Overseas Forces. He stayed in the army following the war and presided over the formation of the Department of National Defence , retiring in 1927. He was a founder of the Canadian Aviation League and commissioner of the RCMP from 1931 until his death at Toronto 5 Mar 1938.

first Canadian aircraft registered after that date and AAB, the second. As a rule an aircraft retained its registration throughout its life, thus those registered before 1929 continued to be recognized by the old designation.

The three day event at Hamilton did not go without incident. The lack of air traffic control proved to be its undoing and there was an accident as Shorty recalled years later. " Fred Shaylor and J.D. Parkinson coming in to land at the same time collided at about 50 feet and crashed together with Parkinson on top in a Pitcairn emerging unhurt. Fred, who was underneath in a Moth spent the next few weeks in hospital".

Not all of the confusion was on the airports. There was much happening in the board rooms of aviation companies and International Airways had already been taken over by a group called the Vickers Syndicate which was headed by Victor M. Drury of Montreal. The Vickers Group amalgamated International with others including Patricia Airways, Interprovincial Airways and a company called Canadian Airways in a controlling entity known as Aviation Corporation of Canada. In time there was further grouping with Western Canada Airways and collectively they became the basis of a grand new nation-wide company which would formally emerge on November 25th, 1930 as single corporation. The owners chose to use the name of one of the smaller companies they had absorbed and it was formally registered as Canadian Airways. The company insignia was a black and white Canada Goose flying with its wings high against a blue background. The whole was encircled by an orange band bearing, in black letters, the words CANADIAN AIRWAYS LIMITED.

A number of the smaller companies had lucrative mail contracts with the government and when it absorbed them Canadian Airways inherited, amongst others, the contracts to fly the mail between Moncton, New Brunswick and Montreal and from Montreal to Detroit, Michigan. The idea was to create a mail service that covered the nation , or at least all of it except the untamed wilderness of Northern Ontario. When fully operational it would carry a letter from coast to coast. The Eastern Division of the company could pick up a letter in Moncton or St John in New Brunswick and carry it over the state of Maine to Montreal, then across Southern Ontario to Detroit, where it would be transferred to U.S. aircraft. The Americans would carry it via Madison Wisconsin, Minneapolis and Fargo to Pembina, ND. There it would be picked up by a Canadian Airways Western Division machine for the short trip north to Winnipeg and then beyond, across the Prairies.

There were also contracts for the mail between Montreal and Rimouski on the south shore of the St. Lawrence and for the winter mail, when the coastal steamers could not operate, along the North Shore of the St. Lawrence to many small communities all the way out to Sept Isles and beyond, and to Anticosti island in the Gulf of St Lawrence.The task of pulling the diverse Eastern companies and contracts together fell to Colonel Redford Henry "Red" Mulock, CBE, DSO, ADC who was appointed to head the company's operating committee. Mulock had been the first Canadian to qualify for a pilot's licence (# 1103) in the British military and by the end of the war had become the highest ranking Canadian in the Royal Air Force. He had worked with Drury in Canadian Vickers, but he admitted that the job of pulling these very different companies together which had, in his words, "gotten into such a mess", was one of the toughest of his career.

While all of this corporate wheeling, dealing and organizing subsequently had a great impact on his life, it must have been of small consequence to Shorty and the other pilots who were kept very busy in that summer of 1929, flying the mail in a variety of aircraft. Two days after his flight from Montreal to Toronto in CATU he made the return trip with three passengers on board in G-CAWB, a Fokker Super Universal. It was a high wing monoplane with an enclosed cabin including room for the pilot and six passengers. Equipped with a 410 horsepower engine it had a cruising speed of 118 miles per hour and that, plus the prevailing tail wind, cut the duration of this flight almost in half. This particular machine had been built under licence by Canadian Vickers Limited in Montreal and was one of many to see Canadian Airways service over the ensuing years, mostly in Western Canada. As the new company consolidated its resources the Fokkers were moved to the west, where for reasons that are not entirely clear, they seemed to have been more popular than they were with the Eastern Division pilots.

Fokker Super Universal
Pratt & Whitney Wasp 410 or 420 hp Engine
Max Speed: 138 mph (222KmH)
Cruise Speed: 118 mph (190 KmH)
Ceiling: 18,000 feet (5,143 M)
Range: 675 miles (1086 KM)
Western Canada Aviation Museum Photo

In the Eastern Division of the company, where Shorty worked, the Fairchild's were the backbone of the fleet. Starting with the FC-2, each different model included improvements over its predecessor and all of them gave lengthy service over the years.

Fairchild FC2
Wright J-5 200 hp Whirlwind engine
Max Speed :122 mph (196 KmH)
Cruise Speed: 103 mph (165 KmH)
Ceiling 13,100 feet (3,740 M)
Range: 600 miles (965 KM)

Fairchild 51
Improved FC2
Wright J-6-9300 hp engine

Photo Courtesy Canada Aviation Museum

The FC-2, like all the Fairchilds, was a high wing monoplane and the pilot sat in the front of a tiny enclosed cabin with a window in front and others at each side barely scraping his elbows. Its design had been influenced by the the aerial survey arm of the Fairchild Corporation and it was often used for photographic work. It had a 200 Horsepower engine and cruised at 103 Miles per Hour.

Fairchild FC-2W-2
Pratt & Whtney Wasp B or C 420 hp engine
Max Speed: 134 mph (215 KmH)
Cruise Speed: 107 mph (172 KmH)
Ceiling: 15,800 feet (4,514 M)
Range: 685 miles (1102 KM)

Fairchild 71, 71B, 71C
(Improved versions increased payload)

Photo Courtesy Canada Aviation Museum ID 6721

The Fairchild FC-2W-2 was an enlarged version of its predecessor with a much more powerful (410 Horsepower) engine and, in its later versions, room for the pilot and six passengers. Its speed was much the same as that of the FC-2. A replica of Canadian Airways Fairchild FC-2W-2, G-CART, is in the National Aviation Museum. Shorty frequently flew the original CART on the Montreal - Toronto and Montreal - Moncton mail runs in 1930.

The Fairchild 71 was a newer version of the FC-2W-2 with similar flying characteristics and payload.

Over the next eight years Shorty was to spend many hours in these machines. In June of that year there were a number of flights between Toronto and Montreal in Fairchild 71's carrying mail.

On 15 July, 1929 he flew another historic flight as the company inaugurated regular air mail service between Toronto and Detroit, Michigan. The flight, loaded with specially marked mail took him from Toronto to Hamilton to London to Windsor and over the river to Dearborn. From then on he was employed almost exclusively on the Toronto - Dearborn (Detroit) run. Throughout the rest of the year he made the flight on an almost daily basis and at least until November, in CF-AAX or CF-ACO, both Fairchild 71's.

These routine 1929 flights called for stops at Hamilton, London and Windsor and occasionally different aircraft were used. Starting in November and continuing for some time many of the daily Toronto-Detroit flights were made in Pitcairn PA-6 Mailwings, G-CAWF and CF- ACT. The Mailwing was an American built plane which had been designed by Harold Pitcairn who held the contract in the United States for the New York - Atlanta mail route and International Airways had purchased a couple of them. Unlike the Fairchilds, which were essentially bush planes, the Pitcairn, with a strong engine and two wings designed for speed was specifically created to carry 500 pounds of mail in the special metal lined compartment ahead of the open cockpit. It was hazardous flying and in spite of considerable economic pressure to make sure that the mail was not delayed it often was, due to bad weather or mechanical problems. For example, Shorty had to make a forced landing in CAWF at Alberton, a small village between Hamilton and Brantford on 13 November, 1929 and again in the same machine on the same route at Rodney on February 4th, 1930.

Pitcairn PA-6 Super Mailwing
Wright J5-9 220 hp engine
Max Speed: 128 mph (206 KmH)
Cruise Speed: 109 mph (175 KmH)
Ceiling: 16,000 feet (4,570 M)
Range: 600 miles (965 KM)
Cargo: 500 lbs
Photo courtesy Canada Aviation Museum

In February he had a chance to try out a new aircraft that de Havilland had brought over from England, the DH 75 Hawk Moth. A high wing monoplane, which looked very much like the Fairchilds, it was designed to carry four people and the British company hoped that it would be as successful as its look-alike. De Havilland had recently moved to Downsview adjacent to the International Airways hangars and there, in between flights, Shorty had run into an old RCAF acquaintance, Geoffrey O'Brian, who had just become sales manager for de Havilland Canada. On February 11th, he persuaded Shorty try out the company demonstrator which still bore its British registration, G-AAFW. In the end the Canadian company was unable to sell any more than three Hawk Moths which saw limited service in the RCAF, but the aircraft was nose-heavy and accident prone and saw very limited use.

Whichever machine he was flying, Shorty found that his night flying experience in 99 Sqn was an asset as a portion of many flights were conducted in darkness. As a rule the pilots would spend the night at the Detroit end of the run at Windsor and then, sometimes as early as 4:30 in the morning, hours before sunrise, particularly in the winter months, fly across the river to Detroit where the mail would be loaded for an immediate take off, still in darkness, for Toronto. With few facilities for weather reporting and even less for forecasting, the pilots would frequently find, when daylight began to emerge, that the ground was shrouded in fog and they would be forced to turn back.

In spite of his busy flying schedule there was time for personal matters and he made many new friends and acquaintances in his life as a civilian. The Montreal area was rapidly becoming the centre of aviation in eastern Canada and a number of companies had established themselves there. The Fairchild Corporation, an American company with a Canadian subsidiary, had a manufacturing element and an air transport element all operating out of its facility at Longuiel on the south shore of the St Lawrence opposite the island of Montreal. There were facilities for both land and seaplanes at Longueil and a number of the companies used the location to transfer from skis to floats or vice versa as the seasons changed.

The companies that formed Canadian Airways operated out of the developing new airport at St Hubert south of the city. In 1927 the federal government had spent $177,000 to purchase 590 acres along the Canadian National track half way between the stations at St Bruno and St Lambert. A further $80,000 had been spent levelling the land and even more government money would be spent on it in the years to come.

Many of these new companies, finding that there were very few Canadian born pilots, had capitalized on the RAF's short service commission policy and had hired pilots, who like Shorty, had reached the end of their military careers but wanted to keep flying. In recent years there have been veiled suggestions that there may have been some prejudice against these "immigrants" and perhaps there was. There always is when the original residents perceive a threat to their livelihood. A young Canadian who had just learned to fly at the local airport would have found it difficult to compete with these accomplished aviators and might well have felt some resentment about "the Limeys" who seemed to be getting the good jobs in the late 1920s. While that attitude may have carried over the years it is difficult to find specific instances when a pilot was held back because of his birthplace. Flying is one endeavour in which the skilled are rewarded for their expertise regardless of personal background. The unskilled rarely survive.

In those early years Shorty was not the only British born pilot and naturally those with similar backgrounds tended to socialize together. Richard Henry "Dick" Bibby, who had won the race at the opening of Hamilton airport, was one who became a close friend. He was a tall, dark Englishman with flashing eyes and a way with the ladies. Many a lass fell to his charm and at least one married lady was known to leave her husband's bed for him, at least temporarily, in a minor scandal that was not particularly well concealed. Walter "Babe" Woollett, also a former Royal Air Force pilot who had come to Canada to work for the Fairchild Corporation, was an exuberant, boisterous fellow. Bernard Martin was another Englishman whose accent and turn of a phrase, (" ba goom lass") revealed his Lancashire birth. E.C. "Ed" Burton had served with the RAF at training schools in Canada and Texas during the war. But there were many others who had been born in Canada. Romeo Vachon who had learned to fly at Grand'mere PQ and Dayton Ohio and then served for a number of years in the Ontario Provincial Air Service, William Herbert "Bill" Irvine and Arthur Ferguson "Peggy" Ingram, with whom Shorty had served in the RCAF at Camp Borden.

Not all of those who became friends were pilots. Horace "Cookie" Cook was employed in the management of Canadian Airways affairs at St Hubert. Over the years he became the company's Purchasing Agent and he and Shorty often served in the same locations. H. Murray Semple, was the Assistant Secretary-Treasurer of the Eastern Division and he and his wife Glad, like Cookie, became life long friends.

There was also Bob Denman, he who had been instrumental in persuading Shorty to join International Airways and who was actively engaged in the negotiations that were creating Canadian Airways. He had married a Hamilton girl, an attractive blue-eyed, sometimes blonde with the most unfeminine name of Douglas and in the fall of 1929 her attractive younger sister. Gwen Glassco, was working as a switchboard operator in his office.

Gwen Glassco

The Glasscos were a close knit family. Four girls, Dougie, Anne, Margie and Gwen were fairly close in age and they were encouraged by their parents to entertain their friends at home in the city or more often at the family farm at Winona in the Niagara Peninsula. Summer weekends in particular often became informal parties around the tennis court and many young friends from the Hamilton area gathered at them. It was to such a party that Denman invited Shorty in the fall of 1929. Perhaps it came as no surprise when Shorty, always the gentleman, asked him later if it would be all right to ask young Gwen out on a date. There were to be many dates that winter and even though they lived many miles apart it seemed to present no problem for a pilot with access to company aircraft. For example on Saturday, November 2nd, his log book reveals that he managed to visit Hamilton, for no apparent reason, in a DH 60 Cirrus Moth, G-CAUA, similar to the Moth he had first flown at Aldergrove in 1925. CAUA now sits proudly in the National Aviation Museum in Ottawa.

G-CAUA
In which Shorty flew from Toronto to Hamilton on 2 November 1929 for a date with Gwen Glassco. It is now in the Canada Aviation Museum, Ottawa
Photo courtesy Canada Aviation Museum

A year later Shorty and Gwen were joined in a marriage that lasted until his death sixty-one years later. It was a big wedding, held, in the tradition of the Glassco family, at Winona on Saturday, June 21, 1930. A few days before Shorty and his best man, Dick Bibby, flew up from Montreal in the Fokker AJF and buzzed the bride and her friends who had gathered at a Burlington lakeshore residence for the bridal shower. Dougie was Gwen's Matron of Honour.

The pilots banded together and gave the young couple a silver cigarette box engraved with all their signatures Many of their names were to become famous in the history of Canadian aviation. (See Annex A) The cigarette box was not an unusual item to grace the young couple's coffee table in those days before smoking was recognized as a health hazard. Most people smoked and when entertaining, the thoughtful host would provide cigarettes for his guests. Nothing could be better to hold them than this silver container which graced the Hatton's home throughout the remainder of Shorty's life. It travelled with them over the years, became slightly battered and the interior scratched by the habit of some guests of striking matches on the inside of the lid. It continues to be treasured by the family even though it is no longer used for its original purpose.

The reception was held at the farm and saw a curious mixture of the Glassco's Hamilton friends with the flyers. It is difficult, so many years later, to describe the glamour that surrounded pilots of all kinds and mail pilots in particular in the late Twenties and early Thirties. The aura that had developed around these modern "knights of the air" in the war had continued in peace time and the growing influence from the United States was making itself felt in Canada. The whole world knew the story of Charles Lindbergh's solo flight across the Atlantic and he was accorded the adulation reserved by a later generation for the first man on the moon. Moving pictures, which were becoming available in every small town, told stories of the gallant fighter pilots singing cheerfully about "the next man to die" and the classic Hollywood line about "sending a kid up in a crate like that" was seen as high drama, rather than high camp. The Americans had made a widely distributed film called "Air Mail" which emphasised the devotion and bravery of these gallant young men who routinely ignored terrible weather and mechanical uncertainty to ensure that the mail got through. These glamourous images embodied in the exotic persons of the suave young Britons had a profound affect on the Hamiltonians and the girls can be forgiven if they found Shorty's friends to be a bit more exciting than some of the fellows next door.

The young newlyweds spent their honeymoon at an exclusive resort, Yama Farms, in the mountains of upstate New York. It was a luxurious establishment to which entry was only gained by an introduction which had been provided by Gwen's sister, Anne, and her husband Charles Henderson. After several days basking in this luxury they went to the new home they had rented in St Lambert, a suburb of Montreal, not far from the St Hubert airport. There they were met by a disturbing surprise: their best man and matron of honour who had been there, together ever since the wedding.

Dougie had fallen hard for Dick, the dashing aviator, and had run off with him, leaving her husband and family at home in Hamilton. She eventually found a small cottage on the shore of Lake Ontario at Bronte, just a few miles east of Hamilton and settled into the life of a single parent while her lover continued to fly the mail.

A Magnificent machine
Stearman 4EM2

Hatton Family Photo

Maritime Mail

It was a magnificent aeroplane with its bright yellow wings, highly polished black fuselage and ROYAL MAIL carefully painted along the side in gleaming white letters. The young Ken Molson, already fascinated by flying machines, could never see enough of it. He would pedal his bike out to the St. Hubert airport when he knew that it might be there on the ground in between mail runs. Years later, as curator of Canada's National Aviation Museum, he made certain that the Stearman 4EM2 was included in the collection of Canada's historic aircraft.

Royal Mail

Postal service as we know it was developed in Great Britain and imported to North America in colonial days.

In Elizabeth I's day and even earlier, letters on affairs of state were carried to and from the Sovereign's court by royally appointed couriers. In 1635, Charles I, in an effort to raise money, allowed the public to use his royal mail couriers for a fee. An Act of Parliament created the Post Office as a government department in England and from then on the terms Post Office and Royal Mail were almost equivalent: the Post Office being the agency that delivered the Royal Mail. The sovereign's mail received priority over that of the ordinary citizen. In 1840, during Queen Victoria's reign, the penny postage stamp was introduced and the Sovereign's mail was stamped and carried like everyone else's. In fact a separate system for the delivery of state mail was developed, but the importance of delivering the mail safely and in as short a time as possible continued. The Royal title merely emphasized the importance. The sovereign's image was often on the stamps and the royal crest on mail boxes. Some ships were designated RMS (Royal Mail Ships) and that distinction gave them priority in berthing on arrival in port. The "Royal Mail" and Royal coat-of-arms printed on the side of Canadian Airways aircraft implied the same sort of priority.

The Stearman was an American creation. Like the Pitcairn Mailwing and the Travel Air BM-4000 it was a single seat biplane but in Shorty's view, "Neither of these two types could could compare with the Stearman aircraft."

With its 420 horsepower engine it could reach a maximum speed of 158 miles per hour, thus making it the fastest plane in the Canadian skies - faster even than the Siskin Fighters that had just come into service in the RCAF. In the early summer of 1930, the newly created Canadian Airways purchased two of them, CF-AMB and CF-AMC. They were shipped by road from Wichita, Kansas and erected at St Hubert by Canadian Airways under the watchful eyes of Stearman technicians. On June 2nd they were accepted by the company and a week later, at a little past 7.00 in the morning of June 11th, Shorty spent about a quarter of an hour in the air getting the feel of AMB. It was a "good feel".

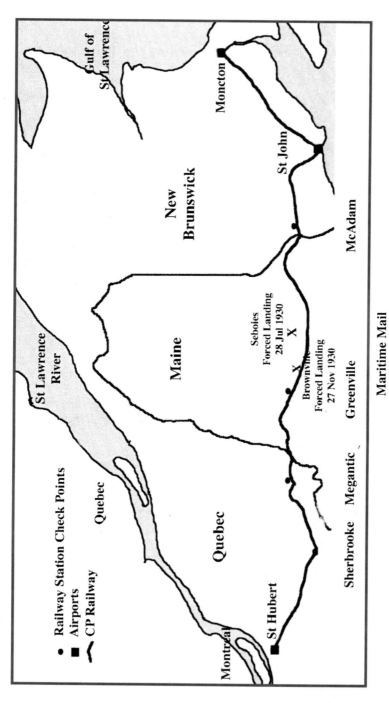

Maritime Mail
"The Bloody Khyber Pass"
St. Hubert - St. John
462 Miles (743 Km)

Years later he was to recall that it was " extremely stable. Stabilizer control was so geared that you could get an extremely fine adjustment on it and in the air you could trim it so that you could fly for quite an appreciable period of time hands off and there was no attempt for error or hunting." A decided asset for the mail pilots who routinely spent two or three hours alone at the controls.

Two hours after his familiarization flight he was airborne in her again, this time loaded with mail for the Maritimes. The trip, which he had completed many times before, was not popular with the pilots. Navigation was achieved by the simple expedient of following the Canadian Pacific Railway line through the dense bush of northern Maine. Arrangements had been made for selected station agents to routinely submit reports of local weather conditions by telegraph to other stations along the line. A system of ground signals using white panels was devised so that the mail pilots flying over could see them. The specific check points along the route from St Hubert to Saint John, New Brunswick were at Sherbrooke and Megantic in Quebec, Greenville, Maine and McAdam, New Brunswick. At each of these stations the pilot looked for the signals which informed him that the weather at the next check point was "good- go ahead"; "bad- turn back" or the one that put the decision in the pilot's hands: "fair - go ahead at own discretion".

The New Stearmans
CF-AMB and CF-AMC shortly after their arrival at St. Hubert in June, 1930. Note the newly installed gas plant for the R-100 dirigible.
Hatton Family Photo

Stearman 4EM2
Pratt & Whitney Wasp 420 hp engine
Max Speed: 158 mph (254 KmH)
Cruise Speed: 128 mph (206 KmH)
Ceiling: 18,000 feet (5142 M)
Range: 645 miles (1038 KM)

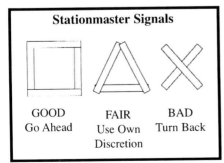

Stationmaster Signals

GOOD — Go Ahead
FAIR — Use Own Discretion
BAD — Turn Back

There were very few places to come down should the occasion arise and Bernard Martin expressed all of their views when he nicknamed the route, "the Bloody

Khyber Pass".

On this trip Shorty was luckier and while not being forced down, he was forced back. Having made it as far as Greenville he saw the station master's signal: a white cross, which meant "Bad -Turn Back" and returned to St Hubert. The next day he completed the flight to Moncton via St John and on the 13th flew AMB back to St Hubert.

Throughout the summer of 1930 he made the Moncton run in a variety of aircraft and not always alone. In the Fairchilds there was nearly always a mechanic (or air engineer as they later became known). Other passengers were formally prohibited but the rule was not strictly observed when it came to company employees or close friends. Although she never grew comfortable with the constant sound of the engine which bothered her ears, Gwen frequently went along, just for the trip. Late in July Shorty fell prey to one of the common hazards of the pilot's upsetting routine and dubious food. He became ill on a trip to the Maritimes and Gwen flew down to Moncton to be with him. On July 28th, with his bride on board it was his turn to run into trouble over Maine. The flight started at 4:20 in the morning in the FC-2W-2, CF-AKT, and the first leg from Moncton to St John was accomplished with ease but on the next leg there were problems. The weather was appalling and the weather signal at MacAdam was a white triangle, leaving the decision up to him. He opted to carry on but, after flying for about an hour and three quarters at 500 feet, he made a forced landing in a potato field near Seboies, Maine, several miles short of the Greenville check point. There they were met by a local farmer who acted the perfect host for his visitors from the sky, fed them chocolate cake and very rich milk and saw to their comfort during their short stay. Gwen felt quite queasy after consuming the rich food but her discomfort probably came from a more basic biological source which would be confirmed nine months later. As the day progressed the weather lifted enough to make another try worthwhile and although the

CF-AKT
The FC-2W-2 in which Shorty and his bride made a forced landing in Maine about a month after their wedding. The aircraft is now on display in the Western Canada Aviation Museum, Winnipeg
Hatton Family Photo

flight was accomplished at 500 feet, they were able to get safely to St Hubert.

In addition to the check points and authorized stops there was another landing field where the pilots knew they could drop in if necessary. Brownville is a few miles east of Greenville and a local potato farmer had left one of his fields uncultivated for the specific use of the aviators. Many of them landed there when the weather was bad and, in late November, 1930, Shorty stayed as a guest for several days. He had been ferrying Canadian Airways only Stearman C-2, G-CARR, to the east on November 27th when engine trouble forced him to land there. It took a couple of days before repairs could be effected and on Sunday, the 30th, after a short local test flight, he made the three hour flight back to Montreal.

G-CARR
On 27 November, 1930, Shorty made a forced landing at Brownville, Maine while flying the mail from Montreal to Moncton in this Stearman C-2.
Photo courtesy the Canada Aviation Museum

While bad weather and unreliable engines frequently resulted in forced landings, one parsimonious practice on the part of pilots was discovered to be another reason. When flying the Fairchilds, which were equipped with two fuel tanks, many pilots had adopted the habit of flying until the engine died as a result of the first tank going dry. It was then a simple matter to switch over to the second tank whereupon the engine usually started up again. Usually, but not always, as Babe Woollett was to discover on Christmas Eve, 1930 while enroute from St John to Montreal with Al Parker as his mechanic in CF-AAX, an FC-2W-2. The engine failed to restart after the tank changeover when they were a few miles short of Greenville, ME. There was no suitable landing place and they crashed into the thick bush and had to walk to the railroad to flag down a passing freight. The aircraft was so badly damaged that it was written off but investigation showed that the engine had failed as a result of a vapour lock preventing fuel from reaching the carburettors. Pilots were immediately instructed to switch fuel tanks before they ran out of gas.

There were many flights to the Maritimes for Shorty that year, some in Fairchilds, others in the new Stearmans and throughout it all great activity at the home base, St Hubert.

In Britain a great experiment was taking place to provide Trans Atlantic air service, using lighter-than-air machines or dirigibles. The R-100 was to complete the North American run and it was decided that St Hubert would be the Canadian base for her. A considerable amount of government money was spent on development of the airport, most of it on a huge mooring mast and a gas generating station, but some on other facilities which would be useful to conventional aircraft. In July the R-100 made its stately way from Cardington, England across the ocean and up the St Lawrence to arrive at St. Hubert on August 1st after a flight of just under 79 hours. As it approached, Montreal went crazy. All the ships in the harbour were "fully dressed" with flags and lights. Hanging from the 22nd floor of the Sun Life Assurance Building downtown, a huge 150 foot long white duck banner greeted the visitors with the message in 30 foot high letters, "WELCOME TO CANADA R-100". It stayed for over a week and on Sunday the 3rd, an estimated 300,000 people went out to St. Hubert to see it. Canadian Airways lost no oppor-

R100
In the late 1920's authorities in Great Britain became convinced that the future of trans-Atlantic travel lay in the use of lighter-than-air flying machines. The government sponsored the development of two airships, the R101 to be designed by the Royal Airship Works and the other, the R100, by a private contractor, Vickers.
Vickers hired two designers whose names would, in later years become famniliar to the public for quite different reasons. Barnes Wallace came to fame during the Second World War as the inventor of the huge "Dam Buster" bombs that were used with such great effect in the Ruhr Valley. That story was told in the movie, "The Dam Busters". Nevile Shute Norway, the other designer, became a writer of fiction. His best-known story, "On The Beach", told of the aftermath of nuclear war and was also made into a popular film.
The R100 could carry 100 passengers in two levels of accomodation. Fourteen 2 berth cabins and eighteen 4 berth cabins were available. It also included a luxury dining room and a two-tier promenade deck with large windows. Since the cruising altitude was to be fairly low at a speed of about 60 miles per hour, the passengers could watch the slow passage of the country below the ship.

Courtesy Airship Heitage Trust, UK

tunity to make a buck or two and Shorty spent the day giving short flights around the airport to a total of 28 paying passengers in ACY, a Fairchild 71.

The R-100 made a short tour around southern Ontario on the 9th and 10th of the month and then on the 13th departed St Hubert for England never to return. On a similar "show and tell" flight in Europe enroute to India in October, her sister ship, the R-101, crashed and burned killing 48 passengers and crew. The British abandoned any further efforts to establish a dirigible service. The expensive tower and the gas plant remained at St Hubert, unused, but the Canadian Airways pilots had no complaints about the new hangars, hard surfaced runways, radios, field lights, meteorological equipment and control tower.

As 1931 approached, Shorty continued to fly the mail to the Maritimes and the newlyweds settled into a comfortable life in their little home in St. Lambert which became a home away from home for many aviation people in the area. Bernard Martin, a vegetarian, dropped by frequently, loaded down with exotic greens such as lentils, to use their kitchen for the preparation of his special dishes. Gwen recalls the day when there was a knock on the door and when she answered there was a young woman standing there, suitcase in hand. She said to Gwen, "I've left home. Can I stay with you?"

Peggy Graham was well known to the Hattons and liked by both of them. She was the step-daughter of one of Canada's pioneer aviators, Stuart Graham, the Civil Aviation Inspector for Eastern Canada.

They took Peggy in and learned that she had had a violent disagreement with her mother. She was to stay with them for some months during which she met and fell in love with one of the aviators. W.H.E. "Bill" Drury had a fascinating background. His mother came from a moneyed family in England who, in a twist on the Lady Chatterly's Lover theme, had run off to Canada with a groom from the family stables. She was not abandoned by her family but became a sort of female version of the classic

> **Stuart Graham OBE AFC**
> Stuart Graham was born in Boston, Massachusetts on 2 September, 1896. He was raised and educated at Truro, Windsor and Wolfville, Nova Scotia. He enlisted in the Canadian army during WWI and spent the winter of 1915 in France as a machine gunner where he was wounded. He then served in the Royal Naval Air Service. He had started flying in the bush in 1919 and then after a brief stint in the RCAF had become, in 1928, one of only two Civil Aviation Inspectors in Canada. In that capacity he was responsible for licensing pilots, air engineers and aircraft east of Ottawa. He also generally supervised civil air operations including search and rescue and he conducted crash investigations.
> During World War II, Graham planned aerodromes and flying facilities across Canada for the British Commonwealth Air Training Plan.
> He died on 17 July, 1976

British "Remittance Man", i.e., a member of the family who was supported financially as long as she stayed out of the country. They operated a farm in the St. Catherines, Ontario, area dedicated to the raising and training of Hackney ponies. There young Bill was raised in an atmosphere of affluence and a complete lack of formal education. His mother did not believe in schools and so he never went to one. When he expressed an interest in flying she bought him a Waco Ten, a very modern, very fast plane, which he promptly learned to fly. He was granted a pilot's licence, (#257) in January 1928 and later that year, on September 12th, he had won a prestigious international air race from Windsor to Los Angeles. Then he moved to the Montreal area, the hub of Canadian aviation, where he operated his one man business.

Bill and Peggy began a tempestuous affair which was hampered somewhat by the fact that he already had a wife. Divorce was almost impossible in Canada and even more difficult in Quebec, where the Roman Catholic Church imposed its notions of morality on everyone, even those of other faiths, and could only be obtained through an Act of Parliament. The young couple finally left for England where they set up housekeeping and, contrary to all the rules of 1930s morality, had two children. When it was possible they married and returned to Canada where Bill resumed his career in aviation.

There was no end of impromptu parties at the Hatton's enlivened by Babe Woollett's collection of phonograph records and, as he was to admit years later, too much drinking.

The phonograph was a fairly new invention and, in an age when there was no television and precious little radio, it was the centre piece of home entertainment. The forerunner of stereo and compact disk systems, it was mechanically powered and produced music from heavy disks on which had been recorded the music of the day, including some numbers that, even in more permissive times, might be considered risqué.

Many of the pilots also belonged to Le Club LeMoyne, an establishment frequented primarily by a French speaking clientele wherein the language difficulties that seemed so important forty years later were non-existent. There was also an unofficial pilot's club at another Montreal night club, Chez Maurice, and to the annoyance of the owner, Phil Maurice, some of the pilots made a gallant effort to live up to their reputations as daring young men by frequently getting into the floor show.

Unfortunately business for the new airline was not as good as had been hoped. The Great Depression, brought on by the stock market crash a year before was beginning to set in. The Americans, who had been purchasing Canadian commodities, started taxing them to the extent that no one would buy. Farmers had been getting $1.60 a bushel for wheat but with no U.S. buyers, the price dropped to pennies. Farmers stopped buying and, with no customers, factories stopped manufacturing. No manufacturing resulted in laid off workers who now had no money thus further reducing the need for manufactured products. With no money for new homes or factories, construction work stopped and the banks called in loans which, in many cases, could not be paid off. Potential users of air services, including the government, decided they could do without.

While the Eastern Division of the company continued to fly the mail there was little other work and, in the West, the government was providing air services in RCAF machines. Services that might have brought in revenue for the struggling company. Canadian Airways was forced to economize by eliminating advertising, letting the aircraft fly a bit longer between engine overhauls and most personal of all, reducing the pilot's base pay from $200 to $125 per month. Still there was money for a Christmas party for the employees and the pilots all gathered in the Mount Royal Hotel for dinner and a "family" portrait on the Saturday before Christmas.

Shorty saw the old year out by flying the mail on New Year's Eve between Montreal and Quebec in a Fairchild 51, G-CANF. The new year was to be less than great from a business point of view. As it turned out flying weather was bad throughout the year and the company was to lose several contracts. All of which must have been worrying to the young couple expecting their first child. Shorty, true to his upbringing, did not believe that pregnancy was the sort of thing discussed by gentlemen. Long after all his colleagues could see for themselves that Gwen was awaiting a "blessed event", he made no mention of it. They, also being gentlemen of the old school, refrained from any comment, at least to Shorty although some of the closer friends had already talked about it with Gwen. Finally, one night when the pilots were together having a few beers and when it seemed to all appearances that the baby was moments away, he quietly took each of his friends aside and, in hushed tones, told them the secret, "Gweno's going to have a baby".

Early in April Gwen's sister, Ann, flew down from Hamilton with Shorty in AKT, an FC-2W-2, to be with her. She was joined in St Lambert by her husband, Chas and on April 11th the Hatton's first child, a daughter, Joyce Gwendolyn, was born. A celebration at the St Lambert home was followed later when Gwen was able to take part, by another great evening at Chez Maurice, where the irrepressible Woollett persuaded the orchestra to serenade her with a popular song of the day, "Here Comes the Mrs".

Friends at St. Lambertt 11 April 1931
Back: Chas. Henderson, Peggy Graham, Shorty Hatton
Front: Bernard Martin, Anne Henderson, H. "Cookie" Cook
Hatton Family Photo

Less than two months later, on 1 June, 1931, the Federal Government, in an effort to save money, cancelled the mail contract for the Montreal - Moncton route.

Night Mail

The "Drunken Duchess" slowed as the pilot boat from Father Point on the south shore of the St Lawrence approached. The Royal Mail Ship, Duchess of Bedford, was known by her less elegant name because of an unfortunate tendency to roll in high seas as a result of her shallow draft. Early in that morning of Saturday, August 29th 1931, she was nearing the completion of her voyage from England but still had a day's sailing before reaching Montreal. As the pilot climbed aboard, mail bags, full of letters from Europe or written by the passengers to friends in Canada, were thrown into the boat and hastily transported to the airport at nearby Rimouski where Shorty stood by a Fairchild 71, CF-ACY. A little less than four hours later he unloaded the mail at St Hubert and the letters went on their way to be delivered at least a day earlier than if they had been mailed after the Duchess docked.

It was not Shorty's first flight to meet an ocean liner nor would it be his last. The very next day he left St Hubert in mid afternoon to deliver last minute mail to the outbound "Duchess of Atholl" as she dropped her pilot at Father Point. In an age when flights across the Atlantic were still pioneering adventures rather than the routine they would eventually become, it was the best that anyone could do to speed up delivery of mail between Canada and Europe.

Not that people were not trying. One company had developed a scheme whereby some ships travelling between Europe and New York carried an aircraft which was catapulted from the deck as soon as they reached a point where there was some certainty of the pilot and his mail reaching shore safely. The German airline, Lufthansa, was experimenting with planes that could land beside ships for refuelling in mid ocean. The papers were full of stories about intrepid aviators

Dutchess of Bedford
Built in 1928 in Glasgow Scotland for Canadian Pacific, London. Capable of carrying 1570 passengers she was employed on the Liverpool - Montreal run throughout the 1930s. Following service as a troopship during the Second World War she was refitted and renamed "Empress of France" in 1947 and returned to the Liverpool - Montreal run. After late 1950s service transporting Canadian troops to NATO duty in Europe, she went to the wreckers in Monmouthshire, Wales in December, 1960.

cutting the time it took to mail a letter from one continent to another.

Earlier the Royal Canadian Air Force, in yet another attempt to justify its existence in an age when all politically correct Canadians knew for a fact that there would never be another war, had experimented with speeding up the overseas mail service. It set up a routine in which the mail was delivered from St Hubert by wheeled aircraft to Rimouski where it was transferred to a flying boat for the cross-Gulf flight to Havre St. Pierre. There it was transferred to a float equipped Bellanca for shipment to Red Bay, Labrador on the Straits of Belle Isle where it would meet the liner. While one or two flights were successful, others were hampered by fog in the Gulf and after a few more attempts, when it became obvious that the uncertain weather could delay, rather than hasten the mail, the plan was abandoned.

A similar experiment had been tried by Canadian Airways on 25 September 1930 when Ken Saunders and Alex Schneider flew two Fairchilds from Montreal and Quebec City to meet the Empress of Australia at Bradore Bay on the Quebec - Labrador Border. They landed the planes alongside the Empress and managed to transfer the mail. They were not so successful the next day when the seas were heavier during their attempt to pick up mail from the Duchess of Bedford and they had to fly back to Quebec empty.

In the spring of 1931 another attempt was made to shorten the overseas mail time when the Empress of Britain made her maiden voyage to Canada. Arrangements were made for her to be met by a tug boat which would rush the mail to Sydney, Nova Scotia. Canadian Airways was to have the two fast Stearman's, AMB and AMC, in place at Sydney from whence they would depart and make the trip to Montreal. Unfortunately Babe Woollett had an accident on landing at Sydney. One of the new Stearmans was damaged when it flipped over on its back during his landing. In any case the tug boat and the Empress missed one another in dense fog. Woollett and Bill Irvine finally had to go back to St Hubert without the mail.

These flights to meet the Trans Atlantic liners were rapidly becoming the only work available for the Canadian Airways pilots. After the loss of the Moncton - Montreal mail service, Shorty had continued to fly the Montreal - Detroit route but on August 15th, the company lost the contract for the section between Montreal and Toronto. For the remainder of that month and on into September flying consisted of the occasional ferry job and a few mail flights to Rimouski to meet ocean liners. On 1 September, while the company managed to avoid laying off any pilots or mechanics, there was another pay cut and some of them were moved to other locations.

Dick Bibby and Babe Woollett had already left the area, having been moved to Winnipeg in June to fly the mail between Pembina, North Dakota and Winnipeg. This short sixty-odd mile flight had, by Canadian regulations, to be flown by Canadian aircraft in spite of the fact that it would have been no problem for the Americans to continue their flights into Winnipeg for that final leg. As a result, Canadian Airways stationed two aircraft and pilots at Winnipeg. From there they took turns popping down to Pembina for the mail and any passengers brave enough to fly in their small aircraft.

Night flying in those days was in its infancy but great steps were being taken to make it a feasible method of operation. In Western Canada an elaborate system of ground beacons had been established to provide the pilots with a visual guide in the dark and airports all across Canada were being fitted with runway lights and beacons. In spite of the fact that pilots had been flying at least part of the route in darkness and in enclosed aircraft, there was a belief that night flying was best accomplished in open cockpit aircraft, from which the pilot could see more easily than from the enclosed cabin of the Fairchilds and Fokkers. With a view to establishing a night mail service Canadian Airways evaluated a British designed mail plane, the Avro 627. Shorty flew it on the Toronto-Detroit run on 2 October, 1931. While it had many good points in the end it was not purchased. Its undercarriage was thought to be too narrow. Perhaps more important, it would necessitate the stocking of English spare parts in addition to those made in North America. Accordingly the company assigned the two Stearmans, AMB and AMC, which were equipped with landing lights and flares, to the Toronto - Detroit mail route. On 19 October, 1931 the route was officially recognized as a night mail run and Shorty was assigned to it.

Since all flying would be out of Toronto he was able to find accommodation for the family in a house at 40 Yonge Boulevard and they left St Lambert. Once settled in the house they were visited by Dougie who, with Bibby settled in Winnipeg, was still living alone at Bronte. She asked that they entertain Bob at dinner, and find out if he would take her back. They did, he did and the Denmans were reunited.

The Stearmans were cold machines in which to fly through the winter night, even though there was insulating material around the cockpit. The pilots had to bundle themselves up in leather fur-lined helmets, goggles, face mask and heavy one-piece flying suits with big boots which made it difficult to feel the controls with the feet.

Landing lights and airport beacons notwithstanding, there was still the problem with weather and the inability to know what it might be a few miles away. Shorty told the story of one late November flight to Detroit in AMB during which he was forced to turn back and return to Toronto in the dark.

In the fall of 1931 Canadian Airways was still using the old Canadian Air Express airport which was located on the east side of Dufferin Street a short distance south of Sheppard Avenue in Toronto. It eventually became part of Canadian Forces Base Downsview but in those days consisted of 220 acres with several buildings and two dirt runways: one running north and south, the other east and west each with drainage ditches along the sides.

"That evening I took off - they put flares down the runway - flare pots to take off and then off I went on my way to Detroit. Hamilton was being rebuilt and having paved runways put in there, so that was completely unfit for any landing, so we just used to pass up Hamilton until it was fit. I was nearly into London over the that ridge of high ground just before you get to London and ran into the most ghastly weather - there was fog and everything so I just couldn't get through . It was right down on the tree tops so I turned and came back to Toronto. In the meantime, the fog had closed in on Toronto also. Of course the airport crew had put out the flares and tucked them away and all gone home. There was the airport completely in the dark and enshrouded in fog. Finally I located the airport by flying up Yonge Street and spotting - at the top end of Yonge Street there was a big - in those days - a big Nielson Chocolate sign - and if you flew west for just another couple of miles there was the airport. Fortunately I was able to pick it out because the one light had been left on - one dim light lighting the wind sock."

Although the aircraft was equipped with flares which could be dropped, Shorty was reluctant to use them because they created disturbing and confusing shadows on the ground. He decided to rely on his landing lights.

"I then proceeded to land trying about three times to just pick out where the runway was and unfortunately the last time I was a little bit off it and caught one of those ditches. And that didn't do much good to the undercarriage. However, by my flying around there, some of the crew who lived close by the airport, heard me and came out. By that time I had climbed out of the aircraft and back up to the hanger . But it took us about twenty minutes to find the aircraft in the dark and the fog that night."

The undercarriage of the aircraft was damaged and for the next few weeks, the night mail between Toronto and Detroit was carried on the one remaining Stearman, AMC.

On Saturday, December, 12th, Shorty had a memorable night in her. The construction work at Hamilton airport was finally finished. It was for the moment, the perfect model of the ideal airport, equipped as it was with perimeter lights, floodlights, and two fully paved runways each nearly 1200 feet long.

There were, in addition, lights to indicate cloud height and to illuminate the wind sock and all were controlled from a central panel in the main office which had telegraph connections to the airports at Windsor, London, Toronto, Kingston and Montreal.

The perfect model of the ideal airport
Hamilton Airport 1931
(Highway 8 (81) in the foreground, Burlington Beach in the distance)
Hatton Family Photo

It seemed to Shorty that all the city had turned out to greet him as he touched down at 6:30 in the black winter evening after the short flight from Toronto. Civic dignitaries and the local postmaster crowded around as the mail for Hamilton was removed from the aircraft and replaced with a bag for points west. He obligingly informed the crowd, including reporters, that the illumination was perfect and that he had no difficulty in landing. Then he was off on the next leg of his trip where things did not go quite as well.

All the city turned out to greet him
Shorty in AMC arrives at Hamilton with the first night airmail
12 December, 1931
Hatton Family Photo

"I was just about at the corner of Lake St Clair around by Tilbury and suddenly a big bang and the flames shooting out of the top of the engine. I landed in a field there and that was that. Investigation showed that an exhaust valve on one of the top cylinders had broken - the valve stem head had parted and fell down in the cylinder and split the cylinder and those were the flames coming out of the cylinder. Anyway we stayed - I took the mail on into Windsor with the postal truck that came out and we replaced the engine . We flew the thing out a couple of days later."

A week later, on December 20th, Ed Burton, flying the same route in AMC ran into fog and became lost. He flew on in a desperate attempt to find an airport and although he could be heard clearly by the people on the ground at Hamilton airport, which was fully lit, he was unable to see anything. Eventually he ran out of fuel and made the agonizing decision to jump. While parachutes had been issued to the pilots for some time, wearing them was not compulsory and there were some who threw them in with the mail in the forward compartment. Not all of the pilots thought highly of this device which was, after all, provided to save their lives. Often they were uncomfortable and there was the concern that an aircraft abandoned in flight could crash into a populated area and kill innocent people on the ground. Anyone who had used his parachute to save his life was said to have joined, "The Caterpillar Club". Fortunately Burton was one of the pilots who had elected to wear his and he survived the jump. While not the first Canadian to save his life with a parachute, he was the first pilot in regular commercial service to do so.

The Caterpillar Club

In 1922, Leslie Irvin, the president of the Irvin Air Chute company made a pledge to donate a gold pin to every person whose life was saved by one of his parachutes. The pin, in the shape of a caterpillar, was made of gold with two red ruby eyes. Starting in the Second World War, the pins were made of gilt instead of the original solid gold.

By 1939 membership had grown to some 4,000 in fifty countries and thousands more became eligible during the war. Records of North American members are kept at the Irvin Aerospace plant in Belleville, Ontario, Canada. Until he died in 1966, Leslie Irvin served as Honorary Secretary of the club. In spite of the fact that he had made more than 300 parachute jumps in his life he never qualified for membership. He never had to jump to save his life.

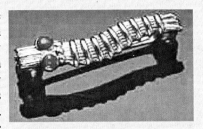

Irvin Aerosspace Photo

The aircraft was not so fortunate. It crashed in an area called McCallum's Marshes near Dunnville where it was found by an Ontario Provincial Police search party the next morning. A postal representative arrived and they managed to salvage the mail but in the process a flare was ignited and set fire to the aircraft. It burned beyond repair and was written off. The company, under considerable pressure from the government to maintain the service on a regular schedule, immediately ordered two new Stearmans which were to be delivered in mid January.

Meanwhile AMB had been repaired and New Years Eve saw Shorty flying her on the Toronto-Detroit run. This time he was not alone. Although the Stearman was a one person plane it was possible to carry a passenger, if the passenger was

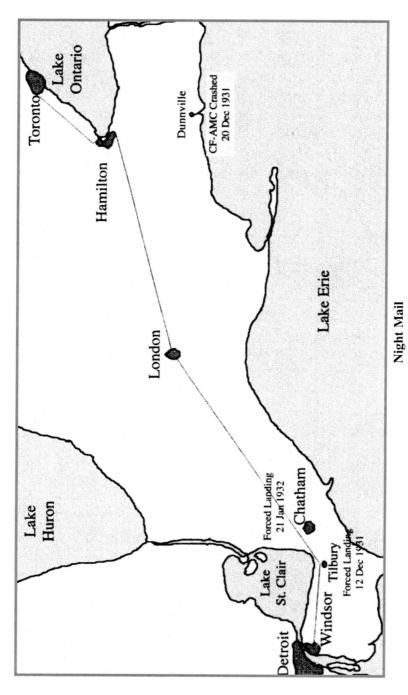

Night Mail
Stearman 4EM
CF-AMB, CF-AMC
October 1931 - April 1932

prepared to be uncomfortable, as he explained in later years. "You could do this by folding back one half of the mail compartment, strapping it down - fasten it down securely and he could sit in front there. Probably would be rather draughty but we have carried them there."

Which is what they did. "Rather than spending New Year's - New Year's Eve and New Year's Day alone in Detroit I decided to take Gwen with me. She would have been at home alone so I tucked her into the front mail compartment of the Stearman and off we started. We landed in Hamilton for a mail change and I was just at the end of the runway before taking off when I got a red signal from the office - from the airport office. So I trundled back to find out what the score was. Apparently an intense icing storm was on its way up from the Windsor district . So we just called it off at that time, which was very fortunate really. That night there was one terrific storm - power lines down all across the Hamilton Beach , trees down - it was really a rather nasty storm."

As a result they saw in the New Year with Gwen's parents at their Hamilton residence where, just a few hours before starting the adventure, they had left their eight month old daughter.

There were other trips on which passengers were carried - usually company people travelling on company business and at least one of them did not think much of sitting in the cold draughty mail compartment.

"One time I was returning a machine having had a forced landing with engine failure and replacing the engine, carrying back the mechanic who was helping. After replacing the engine he had to come back with me but he didn't like to sit in the mail compartment so he elected to sit in the cockpit with me. He sat on the floor with his back to the instrument panel and one leg on either side of the control column and he seemed perfectly happy there. I had plenty of room in the aircraft and that was that."

Thursday, the 21st of January saw another forced landing, this time with considerable damage to the aircraft. Having left Windsor bound for London he experienced engine problems about 15 kilometres east of Chatham and tried to set down in a farm owned by a Frank Stephens. Unfortunately the field was a mass of soft mud, the aircraft wheels sank into the muck and the plane flipped over on its back. While Shorty was not hurt there was some damage to the aircraft and he had to arrange ground transport for the mail.

There was, at that time in Hamilton, an enthusiastic and popular member of the airport staff. Jean Cowman had worked for International Airways and then, starting in 1931, for Canadian Airways as a weather observer and Teletype operator. But she was much more than that. She met and logged every Canadian Airways flight including the night flights in the Stearmans, a task that, at times, entailed being on duty from 5 in the morning to 8:30 at night. She made it her duty to ensure that the mail pilots were met with, not only the latest weather report but also a cheerful smile and a hot cup of coffee. All the pilots knew her and she knew them. She called them, "my boys" and, when it was warranted, she worried about them.

In 1932 she told a writer for Canadian Aviation magazine, "My most exciting moment occurred last January when Shorty Hatton, better known to us as 'Hundred Per Cent Hatton', left London at 7:50 AM. The weather turned bad after Shorty had been up for some time and I prayed often and earnestly during the two hours that I waited, I can tell you. How thankful I was when a long-distance call came in from Pilot Hatton himself. What a relief it was to hear his voice. Of course I had heard him flying above but to see him was impossible. He finally was able to make a forced landing".

Jean Cowman
".... ready formy night Flight Toronto to Detroit. Hopped on a moth about 4:30 p.m. with Dick Proctor as pilot to go aboard the "Stearman" with "Shorty" Hatton"
Hatton Family Photo

Later that winter, in recognition of her service she was granted what she described as "the privilege" of flying with the night mail from Toronto to Wayne, Michigan. She was taken over to Toronto in the afternoon in in a Moth and then, suitably bundled up in a flying suit, made the flight with Shorty. She was later to describe it as "The greatest thrill I had".

Early in the New Year, on 25 Jan 1932, the two new Stearmans, CF-ASE and CF-ASF, were delivered and put into service, but business did not improve and in February all company employees, except the pilots, who had been hit hard the previous fall, suffered a 10% cut in pay. At the same time, for the first time, some pilots and mechanics were laid off. It was to get worse. On March 1st pilots were put on a new system of pay. They were to receive a small base pay plus a bonus for hours flown, a system which further reduced income and most of that dried up two months later when, at the end of April, the government cancelled the Toronto-Windsor mail contract. Shorty had the dubious distinction of flying the last night mail run between Toronto and Detroit.

The effect was devastating on the family which was suddenly dropped from the relatively affluent lifestyle of a glamourous profession to the near poverty of peasants with no income at all. While Shorty was able to pick up some money giving flying lessons at the Montreal Flying Club, "enough to pay for a room and his cigarettes" as Gwen described it, there was no steady income and Gwen, along with the baby, moved in temporarily with her sister Ann Henderson.

Ann's husband, Chas, had been involved in a number of business ventures in and about the Hamilton area prior to the depression but he too had felt the effect and had decided to take up farming on a very small scale. They were renting a house on a farm on the Guelph Line in Burlington where he was endeavouring to make a living raising rabbits. Ann was expecting their second child and Gwen's presence in the house was a godsend. It was a fairly primitive place and when the baby started to come there was no telephone to call the doctor. Gwen had to run down the rural road to the nearest phone and when she described the situation to the doctor he informed her that it was too late to move Ann to the hospital. While the children, one year old Joyce and her three year old cousin Jim were kept out of the way by the new father, John Henderson was born with Gwen's assistance.

Living with relatives was not uncommon. Many people were eking out a livelihood as best they could and there was no such thing as Unemployment Insurance. While some forms of welfare assistance were available, most people viewed accepting them as a fate almost worse than death. Even Bob Denman who, only three years before, had been wheeling and dealing whole aviation companies had lost everything and was dependent on the Glassco girls' Grandmother, Anna Pettit, for accommodation at the Farm. This remarkable woman, liberated generations before there was such a phrase, had outlived two husbands and successfully operated the fruit farm in the Niagara peninsula which she had inherited when her second husband died. Over the years she managed to expand it and operate it as a successful business to say nothing of an enjoyable summer retreat for the family. There were three separate houses on the property. The main house which she had built to include a number of bedrooms was tucked into the woods at the foot of the Niagara Escarpment. It was used as her year round residence and as a summer place for the family. A small house was reserved for the hired man and his family and there was another known as The Tiny House. It was the original farm residence and was usually rented but in these hard times she made it available to the Denmans.

During the depression years "Grannie" Pettit was a source of strength and help, when it was needed, for many members of her family. In those desperate days, the family was often the only hope for many young couples. The older generation, better established in their careers, did what they could do help. Henderson's father, for example, was an agent in the grocery business and while he was not immune to the depression, people did continue to eat. He was able to finance a farm for his son, who made the transition from budding stock broker to chicken farmer. Shorty, with no family in Canada, was not so fortunate but his in-laws provided some help. When there was no money coming in, Gwen and young Joyce lived with her sister in Burlington and later with her parents in Hamilton while Shorty did what he could to earn an honest dollar. It was a long summer and, for the Hattons and many of their relatives, the first taste of the long depression. It was to be another tough seven years before a world war brought any kind of prosperity or financial security.

North Shore Mail

Shorty eased CF-ACO, a Fairchild 71, lower and lower over the Franquelin River just north of the village of the same name. As she slowed and dropped into the valley with the mountains looming on either side, Emile Patraud, just behind him in the aircraft, struggled the mail bag to the window he had just opened and waited for the signal. As they came out of the valley Shorty banked steeply in a sharp right turn, straightened out and then, right over the village, called out to let it go. Patraud pushed the bag out and, before he could get the window closed to shut out the bitterly cold winter slipstream, Shorty made another sharp turn, this time to the left, taking the machine out over the St Lawrence just

North Shore Mail Delivery 1934
From an original black and white wash painting by R..W. Bradford for Avro News, 1952. With Permission

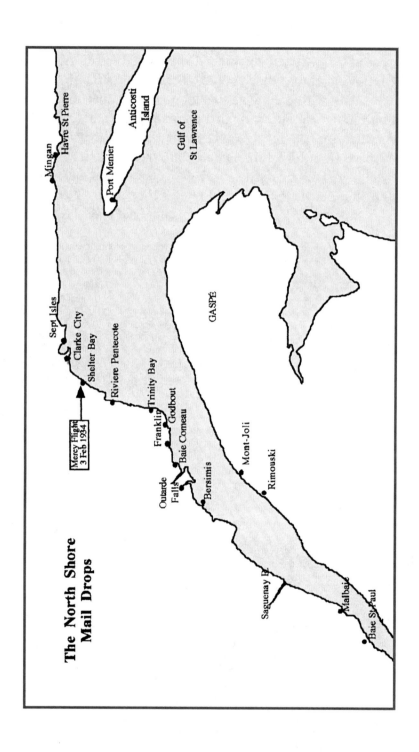

in time to avoid the mountains looming up on the west side of the settlement. Once out over the water another turn to the east pointed them on the next stage of their mail run to the villages along the north shore of the St. Lawrence.

About the only bright light in late 1932 had come in the form of another government contract to fly the winter mail along the North Shore of the St Lawrence. There were a number of communities clinging to the edge of the river and during the summer months they received their supplies and their mail in a coastal steamer. But when the weather was bad and the ice was in the river they had, in the past, been isolated. Several years before the RCAF had begun to provide winter air mail service to these communities and then had handed the contract off to International Airways which first flew it on Christmas Day, 1927. Canadian Airways had inherited it in 1929 but shortly thereafter the government gave it back to the RCAF. Now, starting in the winter of 1932-33, the contract, at very low rates, had been awarded once again to Canadian Airways and the family moved into a hotel in Quebec City to be near the base of operations.

While the notion of whole families living in a hotel would seem unusual in later years, it was a fairly common practice in an age when there were very few, if any, apartments or small homes for rent. In much of Canada, hotels obtained the bulk of their revenue from what was referred to, in government talk, as "licensed premises", i.e., a bar. To obtain that lucrative government licence the operator was required to prove that it was a bona fide hotel by having a specific number of rooms available. Since it was necessary to have the rooms and because there was a limit to the travelling public it made sense to have long-term residents living in them at reasonably low rates. Even in those areas where licensing was not a factor, the practice of having "resident guests" at hotels was not uncommon.

Shorty, Dick Bibby, Babe Woollett, Bill Irvine and others were all employed on this work that winter and for the next few winters. The aviation fraternity all lived in the St Louis Hotel in Quebec City. Although a number of the pilots and mechanics were married there was only one child, Joyce, who stood in great danger of being completely spoiled, so much affection was lavished on her. At Christmas she received no less than twenty dolls, most of which were dispatched to a local Children's Home.

Flights were made twice a week and a typical one, in a Fairchild 71 on skis, would start from the St. Louis Airport at Quebec City and, following the coastline, take the pilot and his mechanic out to Trinity Bay. Along the way, the mechanic would toss the mail sacks out the window as the pilot made the slow low approach over Bersimis, Outardes Falls, Pentecost and Franquelin where it was not possible to land. After a stop at Trinity Bay to drop off the mail and refuel, the flight continued on out to Sept Isles with air drops at Godbout and Shelter Bay. At Sept Isles the mail was divided into two groups: one for the continued journey out along the coast and the other across the Gulf to Port Menier on Anticosti Island. A final stop at Clarke City to spend the night completed the first day. On the following day the flight continued out to Havre St. Pierre. And then there was the return journey.

This business of flinging the mail bags out the side window of the plane was quite exciting and, at times, hazardous. Every pilot who flew the route had his favourite story about it. Dick Bibby, in an article he wrote for Canadair News in 1958, said that the mechanics, who had the job of shoving the mail out the window, routinely made sure that their fingernails were closely pared to ensure that they were not torn off when the wind ripped the canvas bag from their hands. He also told the story about one pilot's attempt to make a more accurate drop at Godbout after complaints had been received from the local postmistress. In an attempt to land the mail bag in the garden of her home, they miscalculated, just a bit, and the bag smashed through her kitchen window.

Even Cookie, who ran the company office at Quebec City during the period of the winter mail service, had his favourite story. In his version one crew, determined to make an accurate delivery, bounced a mail bag off the porch and through the front door which was closed at the time. The door was shattered and the bag burst, scattering letters around the interior of the Post Office. And Babe Woollett had his favourite story, which he recounted in his book, "Have a Banana". He claims that he and his mechanic, Romeo Belanger, managed to drop a mail bag into the back of the mayor's horse-drawn sleigh one Sunday afternoon while his worship was driving it down the main street.

It was during these periodic mail drop flights that Shorty met a man who was to become a fast friend and an honorary "uncle" to the children. Jim Davis was the manager of a paper company at Trinity Bay and although he was not in the aircraft business he was fascinated by the planes and the people who made them work. It was he who turned the business of dropping mail bags into a sporting event. He bet Shorty that he could not drop the bag right into the truck and Shorty took up the bet. Neither of them bothered to tell the truck driver. In a 1963 interview with Harry Goldhar of the Hamilton Spectator, Shorty told how he nearly won the bet

" I signalled my mechanic to let the bag go; it was a good shot. The bag was just about on the truck when the driver elected to get out of the cab to spot where it landed. He had not far to look. As he opened the door the mail bag hit it, took it off, split the mail sack and, I think, the driver swallowed his tobacco."

In the spring of '33, when the mail was once again being delivered by boat, he went back to school, so to speak, and became engaged in some unusual flying, sitting in the dark and trying to make sense of a few very doubtful instruments to ensure that the machine kept on course and in the air. The aircraft was a Puss Moth, RCAF 176, with its side windows blacked out, a second set of instruments installed in the rear and a black drape hung in front of the student's face so he could not see out over the instructor's shoulder. The "blind" pilot was Shorty, a student once again after all those years, and the instructor was Flying Officer Roy Slemon, who in the years to come, would be the RCAF's Chief of the Air Staff and later Deputy Commander of the North American Air Defence System.

DH Puss Moth
Royal Canadian Air Force
Photo courtesy Canada Aviation Museum

In that capacity, in the 1960s, he would become world famous as the man who did not start World War III when all the radars indicated that North America was under a massive missile attack from the Soviet Union. Thinking his way carefully through all of the factors, not just those indicated on the radar screens, he concluded that the political climate was not such for it to be an attack and he put a hold on the nuclear counter stroke that was automatically being set up. He was right. The newly installed radars were reacting to moonrise, not Soviet missiles, and there was no retaliatory nuclear strike.

But in March of 1933, his chief concern was to instruct a group of experienced, "fly by the seat of the pants" pilots in the new art of Instrument Flying. Shorty was one of them, so was Bill Irvine and Babe Woollett who insisted on calling it a Blind Flying Course, "Much closer to the point than referring to it as an instrument flying course". In addition to the three Canadian Airways pilots there were four students from the Department of Transport: Squadron Leader A.T. "Tom" Cowley, Major Robert Dodds, Flight Lieutenant George G. "Baldy" Wakeman and Flying Officer Howard C.Ingram. An eighth student, G.M. Ross, came from the Canadian Flying Clubs Association.

The course had been set up at Camp Borden primarily for experienced

Instrument Flying Course
F.T.S. Borden 1933
Back Row: F/O V.J.Hatton, F/O G.M.Ross, P/O W.H.Irvine, F/O W.Woollett
Front Row: F/O H.C. Ingram, S/L A.T.Cowley, Maj. R. Dobbs MC, F/L G. Wakeman

National Archives of Canada PA-067170

commercial pilots and, aside from the professional qualification, it offered Shorty a brief period on the full pay of his old air force rank, Flying Officer. Students' old military ranks were honoured for the duration of the course and those, such as Bill Irvine, who had no previous air force experience were made temporary Pilot Officers (the lowest RCAF commissioned rank at that time). Thus they enjoyed all the privileges of the Officer's Mess and lived in single officers quarters complete with the services of a batman.

The work consisted of a considerable amount of ground school, including sessions in one of the first flight simulators, a very early version of the Link Trainer. Then there was blind flying by day in the Puss Moth and night flying (blind) in DH 60 Gipsy Moths. It also offered a brief return to the good old days of life in the mess with its tall tales and high jinks over a few drinks on the evenings when there was no flying. Shorty, as usual, was very reserved and proper about the whole thing and Babe, as usual, was just the opposite.

On one such night Shorty had retired after a few drinks but Woollett and a wild RCAF Squadron Leader, Clifford Mackay "Black Mike" McEwen, had partied on. McEwen was a veteran who had destroyed 34 enemy aircraft during the First World War. He would go on to gain a reputation as a stern disciplinarian in the Second as an Air Vice-Marshall commanding the RCAF's 6 Bomber Group, but discipline was apparently not on his mind that evening. Woollett swears it was he who decided that Shorty should not be sleeping alone. Taking an inert 18 Pounder artillery shell that stood by the fireplace, they placed it in his bed with him. Like Queen Victoria, he "was not amused"

Shorty, who never did anything by halves, worked hard, logged a total of 32 hours instrument flying and came second on the course behind Tom Cowley, but like most of the commercial pilots found little practical use for the knowledge gained in his immediate employment. As Babe Woollett later said , "It wasn't wise for us, flying in the bush with no radio, half-assed instruments and no knowledge of what the weather would be at the other end to fly on instruments. So I don't think any of us ever practised it."

Still there was no question that they all enjoyed it and were able to form or continue friendships that would last throughout their careers in aviation. It was a pleasant break in yet another gloomy year and it was followed almost immediately by a tragedy that shocked the Hattons.

**Canadian Airways Pilots and their Instructor
Instrument Flying Course
Camp Borden, Spring 1933**
Bill Irvine, Babe Woollett, F/O Roy Slemon, Shorty Hatton
Hatton Family Photo

Lunch in the hotel dining room on June 17th had been very pleasant, made more so by the presence of Bernard Martin whose good humour was always an asset at any gathering. There had been a bit of laughter and, on Bernard's part, speculation about the blind date Cookie had arranged for him for that evening.

Following the Borden adventure Shorty and Gwen had found a place to live in a small hotel at Longueil. Martin, who had left Canadian Airways and was working for Fairchild just down the road, also lived there. When lunch ended he rushed away to the airport where he was testing a Curtis-Reid Courier, CF-ALM, that had been undergoing some modifications at the Fairchild plant. The owner, G. Algarsson of Montreal, had plans to try a flight across the Atlantic and had brought it into the company to be fitted with long range fuel tanks. Shorty had no flying that day and after lunch he, Gwen and young Joyce returned to their room. A couple of hours later a shaken hotel manager appeared at their door. All he could say at first was, " Mr. Martin.....".

Something had gone drastically wrong during the test flight. The machine caught fire, crashed in flames and Bernard was burned to death. Later when Cookie called to find out why he had failed to show up for their double date, Shorty told him the shocking news and he hurried out to the hotel where, the date forgotten, they made short work of a bottle of gin.

CF-ALM
The Curtis-Reid Rambler in which Bernard Martin was killed when it crashed on 17 June, 1932 at Longueil, P.Q.
Photo Courtesy Canada Aviation Museum

There was other depressing news. Canadian Airways was losing money at an alarming rate, thanks largely to unfulfilled government promises. The company had put out a considerable amount of money to develop air mail facilities on the basis of government contracts. When the government, on very short notice, cancelled those contracts, the bills still had to be paid. The two expensive new Stearmans, ASE and ASF had, for example, been purchased at government urging to maintain the Toronto-Detroit route which the government promptly cancelled. These two magnificent machines went into storage and, except for a brief period in 1936 when ASF was used as a crop duster near Vancouver, were never used again. It is safe to assume that not many owners or employees of Canadian Airways were ardent supporters of R.B.Bennett's Tories. Even the on again-off again service to meet the ocean liners was being flown by the Royal Canadian Air

Force.

There were valiant attempts to recoup some of the costs incurred in the purchase of new equipment and facilities. The recently acquired DH 84 Dragon, CF-APJ, was flown by Ken Saunders out of Cartierville taking paying passengers for joy rides and all across the country company aircraft were used for bush flying. While the jobs were few and far between there was a bit of new business. Mining companies and individual prospectors had always been interested in the use of aircraft and during the winter of 1932-33, lumberjacks became convinced of its effectiveness. Normally they preferred to do their travelling across the St Lawrence by boat, but ice conditions that year were such that the boats were not always able to make the trip. The lumber people found, to their delight, that planes could fly when the boats couldn't sail and from then on the company picked up some business from them.

In spite of these small jobs there were problems with the pay. Pilots received a base pay of $125 per month plus 3 cents per mile and could expect to earn about $300 per month; 400 in a good one. During the winter of 1933/34, in an effort to avoid laying anyone off, the company came up with the idea of pilots sharing their mileage. The idea seemed reasonable and the pilots agreed. Three more pilots were moved to Quebec to share the mail drop flights, making a total of six. It was not until they received their first pay cheques that they realized the company had "shared" the base pay as well. In effect it was a fifty percent cut in pay. Babe Woollett, a bachelor who, unlike Shorty, had no responsibility for the support of a family, blew his stack and told Romeo Vachon what he thought of the plan. Vachon reminded him that the company had lots of pilots and suggested that if he did not like the plan he knew what he could do about it. So he did.

He resigned and went back to England where he stayed for about six months until returning to go to work for Peter Troup who was busy creating a new company which would eventually become Dominion Skyways. In time that company would be purchased by J.R. Richardson and Babe would find himself back in the fold, but that was several years off. To the end of his days he felt strongly about the treatment the pilots received at the hands of the company, "It was shocking for morale, but there was nothing anyone could do about it. The others struggled along. Those who were married were not really in the same position as I was."

Shorty was one of those for whom there was no alternative and he continued to fly his share of of mail runs out to Havre St Pierre, interspersed with bush flying jobs.

By the spring of 1934, with the winter North Shore contract completed the

Company was just about on the ropes and the Directors seriously contemplated closing it down completely. However, after considerable discussion and inconclusive correspondence with the federal government it was agreed to carry on to the bitter end. But not without some changes. The corporate structure was altered and the head office moved to Winnipeg where J.S.Richardson, who had effective control of the company, made his headquarters. Colonel Mulock and Chip Drury both left and promptly joined Canadian Car and Foundry, a manufacturing firm, that was just beginning to look at the aircraft industry.

Later in the year, after more corporate juggling, a new company called Quebec Airways, 75 % of which was owned by Canadian Airways, was formed. Romeo Vachon was appointed Vice-President and Murray Semple Treasurer. The two companies shared offices and other facilities and some members of the staff received part of their pay from one company, the remainder from the other. For all practical purposes from a pilots point of view, it was the same old company. Many of them continued to fly the same planes on the same jobs. Only the insignia on the aircraft changed. The flying goose was replaced by a fleur-de-lis.

Bush Pilot

No matter how hard they tried they could not really make it warm in the canvas covered cabin of CF-AET, but they did whatever was possible for the little girl who lay wrapped up in blankets and winter clothes. The child had grown desperately ill and her father, Dr. Binnett, the local physician at Shelter Bay, recognized the symptoms. Her high fever, severe headache and vomiting had come on so quickly that he knew it was more than the flu. Her dislike of light, her stiff neck and drowsiness convinced him that she had contracted meningitis. At the same time he knew that there was very little he could do for her in his limited clinic which was not much more than a first aid post for the small community clinging to the north shore of the Gulf of St Lawrence, and he had called for help. It came in the form of the Canadian Airways Fairchild 71 which Shorty flew in on the 3rd of February 1934. The aircraft was not designed to be an ambulance but under the circumstances it had to do. Along with his mechanic, he set up the interior of the machine as best they could to keep the little girl comfortable for the long, cold flight to Quebec City. With her father and the mechanic in attendance the plane droned on, its speed reduced by head winds, for 500 kilometres before finally setting down at St Louis field. From there she was rushed to hospital. It was just one of 104 mercy flights carried out by Canadian Airways crews across Canada that year, in this case unsuccessfully. Given the medical knowledge of the day there was little that could be done for the gravely ill child, even in hospital, and she died.

CF-AET
The Fairchild 71 aircraft in which Shorty carried out a mercy flight on 3 February, 1934

Hatton Family Photo

More and more people who had business in the remote north were counting on Canadian

Airways to get them there along with any freight they had. The company advertised a number of regular flights in "large cabin planes" (mostly Fairchild 71s) connecting such remote communities as Senneterre, Rose Lake and Sifton Lake, all mining communities in northern Quebec. J.R. Richardson boasted, "If anybody wanted to fly up the East coast or West coast of Hudson Bay or to Labrador there was no thought of going with any other Company".

Flights of that kind were, of course, very hazardous and, in December 1933, there had been considerable concern when Dick Bibby failed to return from a long flight in CF-AAT, a Fairchild 71, up the east coast of Hudson Bay. Another Canadian Airways pilot, Red Lymburner, eventually found him where he had damaged his undercarriage while making a forced landing at Port Harrison. By early February, after equipment and mechanics were brought in to repair the damage, he was able to fly her out. Bibby's enforced stay in the arctic was not without some small compensation. Furs were very much in vogue in the 1930s and, while at Port Harrison, he was able to obtain at least one dead white fox from the local people which he presented, in its raw state, to Gwen. Shorty took it to the Holt Renfrew store in Quebec where the furriers converted it into a stylish neck piece in the latest fashion.

The company also offered services of "large freighter planes especially suitable for machinery and tonnage shipments" in the Chibougamau and Oskelaneo mining districts. For this type of flying the company used its small fleet of six Junkers W-34 machines. This all-metal low wing monoplane had a 420 horsepower engine and could cruise along comfortably with a heavy load at 100 miles per hour. The pilot sat in the front of the enclosed cabin which had room for passengers but was used more often to carry freight.

Each year in the mid-thirties the tonnages carried by the company increased, but there was stiff competition from smaller companies, some of which had been formed or staffed by former Canadian Airways pilots who, like Babe Woollett, were unhappy with certain company policies. A few of these people managed to undercut Canadian Airways prices by overloading their machines, a practice that was strictly forbidden in the company, and business suffered as a result.

Since many of these flights were in the north in the winter the pilots found their own way of dressing appropriately. Shorty managed to obtain an almost complete "Eskimo" suit in the form of a deerskin parka which hung down to his knees and came with a large hood that completely covered his head. It had been decorated by its native maker with green and red trim and a large "H" on the breast.

Northern Clothing
Shorty in his "Eskimo" outfit
Note the hood covering the aircraft engine
Hatton Family Photo

The outfit was rounded out with mukluks, also made of animal hide under which he wore large duffels made of blanket cloth and socks under them.

This sort of clothing was absolutely essential because, flying as he did from frozen lakes, he never knew what might befall him on the next landing. On one occasion he and his air engineer, Emile Patrault, were forced down on a lake that was covered in drifted snow. While they were able to land without damage to the aircraft, the surface was too rough and snow-covered for a takeoff. Having propped the skis up on cut trees to ensure that they did not freeze to the lake's snow covered surface, they set out to prepare a suitable runway by tying themselves together with a rope adjusted to keep them just the distance between the aircraft's skis apart. For the next several hours, tied together in the bitter cold, they trudged back and forth in the snow pounding it down with their feet to prepare a smooth path for the skis. It worked and finally, after exhausting themselves, they were able to get off safely.

While his records show him to have been a safe pilot who preferred to err on the side of caution he was not always able to make a forced landing when in trouble. Late in the fall of 1935 he and Emile Patrault were inward bound for Quebec City when the weather closed in. A forced landing on the huge river with skis was out of question and they flew on as low as possible, just above the water. There were no major problems until they reached Quebec City where the bridge across the river suddenly loomed up in front of them. Given their altitude and the speed at which the bridge appeared out of the murk the safest course seemed to be under the it. Immediately on successfully getting under the bridge, Shorty had to make a sharp turn to the right coupled with a steep climb to get up over the cliffs that line the river. Once over the high ground it was relatively easy to find the St

Louis airport and they landed safely, just in time to meet Gwen who was arriving by train that day for the winter stay.

They had sub-let their apartment in Montreal, furnished, to a couple in the RCAF and moved for the winter to Quebec where they found accommodation in The Old Holmstead Hotel in the old city just down from the Chateau Frontenac. Overlooking Jacques Cartier Square, the building was reputed to have been Montcalm's headquarters at one time and was in an area with, as Gwen described it, "Lots of atmosphere". Joyce, who was five years old, in an early example of total immersion French language training, was entered in a French kindergarten operated by a Madame Doussault. While she was able, in later years, to upstage her cousins with complete recitations of Sur le pont d'Avignon, there is no evidence that the experience had any long term affect, positive or negative.

In December of that year, the Denmans announced that they intended to spend New Year's in Quebec City and warned the Hattons to line up all their friends for a big party. Bob had apparently landed on his financial feet after the disasters of a few years before and always "the big butter and egg man", as Gwen put it, booked into the Royal Suite at the Chateau Frontenac. From this base in Quebec's grandest hotel they, and many of Shorty and Gwen's friends, attended the New Year's Ball in the Chateau. It was a great party with the ladies in evening gowns and the men in white tie and tails or, at the very least, black tie. A Big Band played all the hits of the day for those who chose to dance in the New Year. The wine ("vinkety-blink Canadian ink") flowed and during the festivities Dougie managed to lose a diamond and sapphire pin. The following morning Bob informed the hotel management which promptly initiated a thorough search. While the pin was never found, hotel staff reported the discovery of three sets of false teeth.

In the early spring of 1936, just before the winter mail runs were scheduled to end, Shorty, with Emile Patrault as mechanic, took a Fairchild, CF-ACO, to Havre St. Pierre. There they met Dick Bibby in another Fairchild, CF-ACY, and during the spring night, the ice went out with a rush. The two aircraft, which had been parked on it at the edge of the shore, went down. They were able to pull both machines out of the water, fold back the wings and start the two-day process of drying them out.

Drowned Fairchilds
CF-ACO and CF-ACY drying out after their soaking when the ice
went out at Havre St. Pierre, 1936

Hatton Family Photo

While it was not an easy task, it was made easier by the fact that both machines had been prepared for the cold overnight stay in the routine followed by all bush pilots. When shutting down the night before, the supply of fuel to the engines from the tanks had been cut off and the engines run until they stopped, thus ensuring that the carburettors were clear of any gasoline. The engine oil had been drained and taken , in five gallon cans, indoors where it could be maintained at some degree of warmth and viscosity. In really remote locations, where the only crew accommodation was a small tent, room was always made for the engine oil along with the pilot and mechanic. The engines were then covered for the night with a "nose hangar" which was nothing more than a canvas tent draped over the engine to protect it from the elements. In the morning it was normal procedure to warm the engine oil, usually over a fire and, at the same time apply a blow torch to the engine block inside its tent. When both oil and engine were warm enough, the oil was added, the tent removed and gasoline was pumped into the carburettor for a quick engine start before it had a chance to cool down.

Years later Shorty described the next step to a reporter from the Hamilton Spectator. " The next problem was to take off, since all the heavy ice had gone out and the shell ice, naturally, would not hold an aircraft. To take off we moved the two aircraft on to high spots on the shore and headed them towards the bay. We next recruited a number of villagers to chop up large blocks of ice and build us a long inclined ramp from the aircraft down to the sand of the bay. Then, at low tide, with the shell ice resting right on the sand, we started up, slid down the ramp and had enough speed to keep going and make a successful takeoff".

Shortly after that adventure, the winter mail run ended for the season, the Hattons moved back to their apartment on Cote de Neiges in Montreal and on July 17th, their second child, another girl, Suzanne Josephine, was born at the Royal Victoria Hospital.

Early in 1936 the Department of National Defence, which was still the government agency in charge of civil aviation, initiated the Canadian Transport Pilot's Licence. While it called for expertise in instrument flying, there was some confusion as to exactly what that meant. Many Canadian Airways pilots had, like Shorty, taken the RCAF "Blind Flying" course at Camp Borden but, in some cases at least, this apparently was not good enough. Such was not the case with Shorty whose application was approved and on 4 April 1936, he was issued licence No. 16. It was identical to the one he had been issued in London in 1928 except that in this case it was signed by a Canadian and a fellow student on the 1933 RCAF Instrument course at Camp Borden. Tom Cowley had been promoted and, in his new job, signed Shorty's licence, "A.T.Cowley, W/C, Superintendent, Air Regulations". Initially it licensed him to fly "single engine landplanes & seaplanes" and the "D.H.84" for the public transport of passengers, mail or goods and for industrial purposes but it contained space for the addition of other aircraft in the future.

The introduction of this new licence, which called for a written examination, created a problem for one of Shorty's colleagues. Bill and Peg Drury, now married, had returned from England and Bill was working, once again, as an independent operator flying his Waco, often on jobs for Dominion Skyways. Although his marital status had been legitimized he still suffered from what would be known in later years as "adult illiteracy". Because his mother had never sent him to school he had never learned to read or write. Faced with a written exam he had a problem which was solved by his father-in-law, Stuart Graham, the Civil Aviation Inspector in Eastern Canada. Graham agreed to oversee an examination in which his daughter, Peggy, read the questions to her husband and then wrote down his answers. The Drury's passed the test, Bill was granted one of the new licences and continued flying.

In October, the family was on the move again, this time to Rimouski, which had replaced Quebec City as the base for North Shore operations and from which Shorty would be operating over the winter of 1936-37. They made the trip in a Dragon Rapide, which Gwen will never forget since it bore Shorty's initials "VJ".

A year before the company had purchased two of De Haviland's newest machines, DH 89 Dragon Rapides. A twin engine fabric-covered biplane with an enclosed cabin providing room for the pilot and eight passengers, the Rapide was in service in Britain and several modifications were included in the machines produced for use in Canada. Special arrangements were made for the installation of floats or skis and the engines included a quick drain facility so that the oil could be removed rapidly on overnight stops when the weather was bitterly cold. It was designed as a small airliner and it was for this purpose on the Vancouver-Seattle service CF-AEO and CF-AVJ had been bought.

DH 89 Dragon Rapide
Engines: Two DH Gypsy Six
200 hp
Speed: Max 157 mph (252KmH)
Speed: Cruise 132 mph (212 KmH)
Ceiling: 19,500 feet (5570 M)
Range 578 miles (930 Km)
Hatton Family Photo

The Rapide has been described as "the poor man's airliner" and unfortunately an American company, United, was using a much more modern aircraft, the Boeing 247, over the same route. A Canadian Airways official noted that the Rapide "looked rather silly" by comparison. Eventually the company acquired Lockheed Electras for the Vancouver - Seattle route. At the same time concern was being expressed about the practice of flying single engine aircraft over long expanses of open water, such as the Gulf of St Lawrence. It was deemed prudent to use twin engined machines on such flights and the Rapide, AVJ, was transferred back east to be used on the mail runs out of Rimouski which routinely crossed the water to the North Shore and out to Anticosti Island. While a number of communities along the North Shore had managed to build small landing fields for the mail planes there were still some where it was necessary to continue the practice of dropping the mail bags from the plane as it flew low over the village. To facilitate this, a special mail chute was built into the floor in the rear of the cabin. The mechanic had to open the trap door and when he received a signal from the pilot on a buzzer system he pushed the bags out. One mechanic, on his first trip, was so anxious to get the bags out quickly that he opened the door and inserted the first bag in the opening a bit early. Unfortunately the slip stream grabbed the bag and the mechanic almost went with it as he desperately hung on until receiving the signal to let go.

Gwen never forgot that October move for another reason. She had bundled the family, five year old Joyce and the three month old baby Sue, aboard and, with Emile Patrault in attendance, Shorty completed the flight from Montreal to Rimouski where the winds were unusually high. So high in fact that, twice as he made his approach, he had difficulty getting the relatively light machine down, deemed it unwise to land and went around again. As he was getting ready for the third attempt, Emile leaned over to Gwen, touched her on the shoulder and said, "Don't worry Mrs., he's very good". Shorty proved him right by setting the machine down in a perfect landing.

Having settled the family in Rimouski, Shorty immediately had to leave them for a month while he returned to Montreal to take another Instrument Flying Course.

The company had been concerned about the ability of its pilots to meet commercial airline standards for some time and that, coupled with the Department of National Defence's vague requirements for instrument qualifications, had prompted it to set up a course of its own. Early in the year it had sent one of its pilots, Z.L. "Lewie" Leigh, to California to attend an instrument course at the Boeing School of Aeronautics. After completing the course, Leigh had returned to Canada and arranged to have two aircraft fitted for Instrument instruction. Laird LC-200 two-place biplanes, CF-AQY and CF-APY, were fitted with two sets of new instruments each and a folding canvas hood over the front cockpit from which the students could fly

CF-APY

One of the two Laird LC-200 aircraft used in the Canadian Airways Instrument Course, 1936.

Western Canadian Airways, before being absorbed by Canadian Airways purchased four Laird aircraft in 1931. Two of them were destroyed in a fire shortly after they were received. CF APY was sold in 1940 to Johannesson Flying Service of Winnipeg which operated it until 1943 when it was purchasd by a buyer in Hamilton where it was placed in storage.

Photo and information courtesy Brian Johanneson

"blind" under the watchful eye of the instructor in the rear cockpit. Leigh took his mobile flying school to several Canadian Airways bases in Western Canada over the summer and conducted his course for a number of company pilots. In November he set up shop at St Hubert and over the next couple of months trained Shorty, Romeo Vachon, Freddie Bone, Dave Imrie and Red Lymburner in the intricacies of flying on instruments and radio range procedures. Imrie and Lymburner were products of Canadian Airways policy of helping their employees advance themselves. Both had joined the company as mechanics and had been trained as pilots on the job. They all stayed in a boarding house at Longuiel and spent part of each day and many nights in the air under the hood of AQY. In the end they were tested by Stuart Graham, still the Civil Aviation Inspector for eastern Canada. Once again Shorty demonstrated his skill and zeal and passed Graham's examination after slightly less than nine hours in the air. He was able to return to the family at Rimouski in time for Christmas.

This time, for a change, they had not taken accommodation in a hotel but had managed to find a house to rent. It adjoined a local hotel and was owned by the hotel operator who continued to occupy a front room by the entrance which he had set up as an office. He had also made arrangements to continue to use the basement for the storage of extras from the hotel. The Hattons had met and become friends of the local Royal Canadian Mounted Police constable who came to the door one day with a grim face and the news that he was not making a social call. The landlord was using his part of the house for a lucrative bootlegging operation.

On 17 December, 1936 Shorty opened the winter service along the St. Lawrence River. His flight from from Rimouski with specially annotated mail for Havre St. Pierre, Natashquan and Harrington Harbour formally inaugurated the new service. In two other historic flights one on Christmas Day, 1936 he carried the mail from Rimouski to Port Menier on Anticosti Island and on 30 December he flew the reverse route. In both of these flights the mail was specially marked.

It was a long winter and for much of it the road out to the airport was blocked with snow. On flying days Shorty would make the trip to work on a novelty of the time, one of the first snowmobiles built by Bombardier of Quebec City. Gwen recalls how he would head out to work in the morning, " I would pack Shorty and Emile Patrault's lunches and two large thermos's of consomme laced with sherry, which was very welcome as there was no heat in the aircraft".

The Canadian Airways base at Rimouski had first been established in 1932 and by this time it was a going concern, complete with a well-equipped workshop in which the mechanics could work on aircraft overnight to avoid the loss of precious daylight flying hours. There were also radios linking the aircraft with stations on both the north and south shore and they operated on frequencies which could be picked up by the commercial radios owned by most families. When they were not listening to such popular programmes as Jack Benny or Charlie McCarthy, Gwen and the girls could hear the different stations on the net and and learn which towns Shorty was flying over.

There was excitement and change in the air that winter and on into the summer of 1937. Shorty's principal duties were flying the Rapide to the North shore or providing the company's advertised services between Montreal and Father Point (Rimouski) carrying "mail, passengers and express....to connect with incoming and outgoing Canadian Pacific mail steamships". Wherever he went, one subject always came up in the conversation. For several years, the aviation community had been preoccupied with a plan that would provide new opportunities for the flying fraternity and now it seemed to be nearing fruition. The status of a new national air line was on everyone's mind.

The National Airline

The scenery, which was magnificent at times, eventually became nothing but tree upon tree, many leafless with the first traces of snow on the branches, going on, it seemed, for ever. It was a long trip by train, but it was the only practical way of moving to the West in the late fall of 1937. Up the Ottawa from Montreal across to Sudbury and then north through the never ending bush and past the tiny communities with their unlikely names - Hornepayne - Fire River - in the rattling cars of the transcontinental railway with their apparently uneven wheels clanking on the roughest road bed in the world. The little girls, Joyce at six and Sue not quite two, grew restless and cranky, bored with their colouring books and the confinement. It was not much better for the adults but the train trip from Montreal to Winnipeg was made bearable for the family by the thought that it was taking them to a new life working for the recently created Trans Canada Airlines.

Throughout the Thirties there had been much tug and tussle in Canada over the development of a national air line that could provide passenger service from coast-to-coast. There was considerable discussion between Canadian Pacific Railways and the Minister of Transport, C.D. Howe, about the composition of a new company. Howe was a powerful member of the Mackenzie King cabinet who was to become even more powerful in the years to come. During the preliminary discussions, Canadian Airways had allied itself with CP and had developed fairly extensive plans for the new airline which were submitted to Ottawa in September, 1936.

In the end, CP found it impossible to commit itself to the project without greater control than that being offered by Howe and withdrew from further participation in the project. On 6 April, 1937 the Bill creating Trans-Canada Airlines without Canadian Pacific or Canadian Airways participation was passed in Parliament. Canadian Airways experienced some difficulty in having its plans for the airline returned and was shocked to learn that some senior officers who had worked on them were joining the new company. Eventually the plans were returned and Canadian Airways accepted the fact that many of its pilots and mechanics would leave to join the new company. Arrangements were made for them to join TCA with sufficient notice to ensure Canadian Airways continued operations.

On 20 August, Lewie Leigh, who had run the Canadian Airways Instrument Course the previous winter, was hired as the new airline's first pilot.

He immediately put out word to his Canadian Airways colleagues, particularly those whose instrument flying he had checked, that TCA was hiring. It was an attractive proposition. A captain's salary at the time was $400 per month and, truly appealing was the fact that it was every month. No more base pay plus pay for air time, or worse, flying pay only. This was to be a salary guaranteed in fair weather or foul. And a pretty reasonable salary it was in a time when cigarettes were a penny apiece, coffee was 25 cents a pound, a couple could take in a movie for 40 cents, a man could buy a suit for 12 dollars and a four bedroom apartment could be rented for 25 dollars a month. Many Canadian Airways pilots, including Shorty applied for the jobs.

As TCA began to take shape a number of senior executives were hired from US companies and orders were placed for aircraft, specifically Lockheed 10A Electras. Two were acquired from Canadian Airways where they had been used on the west coast and three others were ordered from Lockheed. The Electra had been developed by Lockheed for airlines that intended to carry a small number of passengers. A low wing, twin engine monoplane it had accommodation for a crew of two and ten passengers in an all metal fuselage. Modern improvements included retractable landing gear and variable pitch propellers. A variation of the 10A, the 10E became world famous when Amelia Earhart was lost in one on her fatal attempt to fly around the world in 1937.

Lockheed 10A Electra
Engines: Two Pratt & Whitney Wasp Jr.
400 hp
Speed : Max 190 mph (305 KmH)
Speed: Cruise 180 mph (290 KmH)
Ceiling: 21,150 feet (6,042 M)
Range: 850 miles (1,368 Km)

Note: This aircraft was originally CF- TCC. It is now in the Canada Aviation Museum, Ottawa
Photo Courtesy Canada Aviation Museum

In October, a training school was established in the old Canadian Airways building at Winnipeg's Stevenson Field under the direction of Chief Instructor W.A. "Bill" Straith who had come to the company from Northwest Airlines in the USA. All newly hired pilots were required to undergo an extensive period of flying instruction, the main feature of which was instrument flying in three Electras, CF-BAF, CF-TCB and CF-TCC. This latter machine, now bearing the registration

CF-TCA is in the National Aviation Museum at Ottawa.

The Hattons found accommodation in a boarding house on Winnipeg's Broadway Avenue, Joyce was enrolled in a local school and Shorty went, each day, out to Stevenson Field to take the course. They explored Winnipeg, discovered, as so many Canadians have before and since, just how cold it can be on Portage Avenue with the wind whistling in from the prairies and prepared to stay.

Gwen cannot forget the day when, after several wintry weeks on the course which was apparently going well, Shorty arrived home from work - she was bathing the kids - and said to her, "They've let me out".

As a seasoned pilot he struggled to understand what had happened. He had been flying one of the Electras with Straith in the other seat and during the course of the flight, while Shorty was concentrating on flying the machine, Straith kept poking him, apparently trying to distract his attention. On landing Straith took him aside and told him that his reflexes were not fast enough for TCA. It was a criticism that was new to him and, as an experienced instructor, he was puzzled by the curious technique of instruction. As it turned out, Straith did not last long with TCA and returned to the USA where, several years later he was killed in a flying accident.

Of the five pilots who had taken the Canadian Airways Instrument Course in December, 1936, only two, Romeo Vachon and Dave Imrie, were hired by TCA. A year later, Imrie was killed when the TCA Electra he was flying from Winnipeg to Vancouver caught fire and crashed at Regina.

The end of his short career with Canada's national airline came as a severe blow to Shorty's ego to say nothing of the adverse effect it had on his financial situation. He was out of work in Winnipeg with no job prospects in that part of the country. To make matters worse, everyone in the family picked up a bug and they had to make the interminable train journey back east with everyone sick and miserable.

When they arrived in Montreal, Canadian Airways, which had no reservations about his skill as a pilot, was delighted to take him back. The company had purchased a new Dragon Rapide, CF-BFL, in October and was offering twice-a-week regular flights from Rimouski along the North Shore. The Hattons got some of their furniture out of storage and moved back to Rimouski, this time avoiding the bootlegging establishment in which they had lived earlier.

They celebrated a quiet Christmas at the St. Laurent Hotel in Rimouski and then, just before New Year's, a face from the past appeared in the hotel. Babe Woollett arrived one afternoon in a Fairchild 82 with a load of passengers, their equipment and a fantastic story. He had been engaged for about a month surveying Anticosti Island on a special contract arranged by a Dutch company which had explained that they were interested in the forestry industry and were looking into the possibility of buying the whole island. When the company experts arrived it became obvious that they were not Dutch and not one of them had any noticeable skills in the pulpwood business. Two were officers in the Luftwaffe, the German Air Force, one was in the Wermacht, the German Army and the fourth was a German Naval Captain. After completing the survey they had thrown a huge Christmas party, complete with a tree covered in German decorations, at Port Menier. During it they made sure that every local citizen received an elaborate gift from their apparently inexhaustible supply of Scotch and engraved wrist watches. All of which was accomplished with the strains of "Stille Nacht, heilige Nacht" playing quietly on a gramophone in the background.

On their arrival at Rimouski in bad weather they had hastily loaded their newly marked maps and aerial photos onto the train and departed, leaving Woollett and his mechanic to wait out the weather in the St Laurent Hotel. Woollett was able to fly to Montreal the following day where he reported his clients unusual activities to the authorities, but their real significance did not become fully apparent until several years later when, during World War II, Nazi submarines frequently operated quite comfortably in the waters surrounding Anticosti Island.

While Shorty's failure in Winnipeg must have been a blow at the time, it was probably a blessing in disguise. Had he been hired as a TCA pilot he would undoubtedly have spent the rest of his flying career in a neat uniform, carrying passengers on almost automatic, routine flights between depressingly similar airports. While it offered a stable financial situation, it did not, perhaps, lend itself to the exploration of the unknown that had characterized his life since he was a boy. As it was, his career took a quite different turn. Little did he know, when he left TCA, that a third of his flying career was ahead of him. A period when he would be the first to fly some of the most modern aircraft of the day.

The End of an Era

It was stifling in the small room at the St Laurent Hotel in Rimouski but at times Shorty shivered with the cold. An hour later he would be burning up. He had never fully recovered from the illness that plagued the whole family on the trip from Winnipeg and seemed to have developed a very bad cold that settled in his chest and caused him to have difficulty breathing. In addition there were the alarming fevers and chills that gripped him from time to time. The local doctor came and diagnosed a cold, but Gwen was not so sure. This seemed much worse than any cold she had ever seen. She confided in a friend, Beryl Palaisey, a nurse and the wife of the Canadian Airways Chief Mechanic in the area. Beryl took one look at the patient and immediately recognized pneumonia. For the next month she and Gwen nursed him back to health.

Then, late in that spring of 1938, too late as it turned out, he had an adventure which he always swore was the sure cure for what had ailed him. A number of natives, living in the unmapped bush north of Havre St Pierre had been discovered near death from starvation. An operation was mounted to drop food to them and when Shorty left home there was no way of knowing how long it would take. After six days with no word from him, Gwen began to worry but tried to hide her concern from the children and the neighbours.

She was not entirely successful, "The Nuns from the Church visited and wanted to know if they could say some prayers".

Perhaps their prayers helped. On one flight into the unmapped country in a Fairchild the weather had turned bad and Shorty decided that a forced landing on one of the lakes below was in order. The first part of the landing went well, but as the machine slowed down he realized that the surface was covered, not in solid ice, as it appeared but wet slush. The slush grabbed the skis, arresting forward movement and the front end dipped down immersing the engine in the mixture of icy cold water, ice and soft snow. His mechanic on this trip was Emile Patrault and, once again, as they had been in the spring of 1936,

Émile Patrault

Emile Patraud was born in 1907. His first job in 1924 was as a mechanic in Roberval for Dominion Aerial Exploration Co. He then worked at Lac-à-la-Tortue for Fairchild Aviation, before joining Canadian Airways. He entered Trans-Canada Air Lines (later Air Canada) in 1938 and, in 1947, became the first French-Canadian to be appointed Regional Supervisor of Maintenance in Toronto (TCA's largest base). He retired from Air Canada in 1968 and died in 2000. In 2002 he became a member of the Quebec Aviation Hall of Fame.

they were faced with the problem of getting the machine out of the water and drying out the engine. Only this time they were alone and it proved to be a daunting task. Working as a team, the two men managed to right the aircraft, then drain and partly dismantle the engine to dry the individual parts over a small fire. Much of the detailed work on the engine had to be done without gloves and their bare fingers were skinned and frozen. Fortunately the weather turned colder and though it did not add to their comfort it did freeze the surface of the lake so that by the time they had dried and assembled the engine it was possible to make a successful take-off.

Another problem arose when Tom Mahon flying the new Rapide, BFL, crashed at Matane, PQ on February 23rd. The aircraft was a writeoff and Mahon was injured. As a result Shorty and AVJ had to do double duty maintaining the company's regularly scheduled flights out of Rimouski. He spent very little time at home for the remainder of that winter and logged many hours on the long flights across the St Lawrence and along its North Shore. During this period he set a local record for endurance flying when he went from Rimouski out to Havre St Pierre and back in one day.

The company was now facing unprecedented tough times. In 1938 the volume of freight decreased by 32 % and it was obvious that the loss of the contest to operate the national airline had taken its toll. Not that Canadian Airways was dead. It continued to purchase new planes with a view to continuing bush flying and in the spring the family moved back to the Montreal area. There they found a house in St Lambert, from which Shorty took the trolley each day to the office where much of his work at that time was concentrated.

While he continued to fly commercial jobs some of his work involved testing and the acceptance of new aircraft from the factory. May 18th found him at Fairchild's Longueil facility testing CF-ACY, a Fairchild 71 that had been in the company for several years but had just been fitted with floats. On the 28th and 29th of May he flew the newly built

CF-BKP
Shorty accepted this Fairchild 71 from the factory for Canadian Airways on 28 May, 1938 and ferried it to Winnipeg
Photo Courtesy Canada Aviation Museum

Fairchild 71, CF-BKP, accepted it on behalf of the company and ferried it from St Hubert to Winnipeg via Hamilton, Madison, Minneapolis, Fargo and Pembina.

On June 16th Canadian Airways purchased a new Norseman IV, CF-BDF, from the Noorduyn plant at Cartierville and Shorty conducted the acceptance tests. Later that summer the company replaced the Rapide that had been lost during the winter at Matane. CF-AYE was of the same vintage as the other Rapides in the Canadian Airways fleet but had been used as a demonstrator by de Havilland since its arrival from England. In 1936, they had used it to test some newly designed skis which never went into production and later that year it had figured in the Moose River mine disaster near Halifax, NS. In this much publicized event, several men had been trapped in the collapse of the mine and a number of attempts were made to rescue them. Included in the plans was an effort to to lower a radium capsule through a hole into the mine to help the rescuers keep direction and AYE was used to transport the radium from Toronto to Halifax. The trapped men were eventually rescued and de Havilland did not suffer from the publicity.

Noorduyn Norseman IV
Engine: Pratt & Whitney Wasp
Speed: Max 170 mph (273 KmH)
Speed: Cruise 150 mph (246 KmH)
Ceiling 22,000 feet (6258 M)
Range: 600 miles (965 KM)
Note: Shorty conducted the acceptance tests on this machine (CF-BDF) on 16 June, 1938 on behalf of Canadian Airways
Photo Courtesy Canada Aviation Museum

On the 27th of June, 1938, CF-AYE was in St Hubert where Shorty checked it out in a brief local flight and then in a two and a half hour trip he ferried it to Toronto, the site of the de Havilland factory. To round out a very full day he returned to Montreal that afternoon with a short stop at Trenton in the company owned DH 84, CF-APJ which had been undergoing an overhaul at the factory. CF-AYE was formally acquired by Canadian Airways on 5 September, 1938, two months after Shorty ferried it back de Havilland.

There was a bit of flying in the last half of July, including several mail runs to Rimouski in CF-BBC, another Dragon Rapide. Early in August, he made a short local flight in the Montreal area in AVJ, the Rapide identified by his initials which held such shaky memories for the family after their 1936 flight in it to Rimouski.

He spent most of August, 1938 operating from the Canadian Airways base at Senneterre in Northern Quebec. The company had established the base in earlier years to serve the new mines that were opening up in the Chibougama area and, following J.R.Richardson's acquisition of Dominion Skyways, had just combined it with the one operated by that company. It was a fairly primitive bush camp with several small cabins serving as freight sheds and living quarters.

Several flights in the company's Junkers W-34, CF-ATF, on floats between Senneterre and Ross Lake were followed by a rather lengthy flight when he ferried ATF from Senneterre to Toronto via Orillia, Ontario on August 12th. While he was struggling with the door at the refuelling stop at Orillia the ladder, which was carried inside the aircraft, slipped and fell into the waters of Lake Couchiching, where, presumably, it rests to this day. ATF had been purchased by Canadian Airways in 1932 and, having served a number of owners, finally retired to the National Aviation Museum in 1962 where it is now displayed, complete with a new ladder.

**Junkers W-34
(CF-ATF)**
Engine: Pratt & Whitney Wasp C 420 hp
Speed: Max 125 mph (201 KmH)
Speed: Cruise 100 mph (161 KmH)
Ceiling: 13,500 feet (3857 M)
Range: 490 miles (788 KM)
Photo Courtesy Canada AviationMuseum

The remainder of August was filled with short flights carrying passengers and freight from Senneterre to Fish Lake, Cameron Lake, Lac Laverdier and Lac Gueguer. These jobs were carried out in a number of different machines; CF-APG, a DH 83C Fox Moth owned by Canadian Airways and two Dominion Skyways planes: CF-AWU, a Fairchild 71 and CF-AHG an FC2-W-2.

They were his last flights for Canadian Airways which he had joined on its formation eight years before. Over those years he had added thousands of hours to his log book under flying conditions that were, at best, uncomfortable and often hazardous. He had risked his life innumerable times on flights that would be considered dangerous today but which he viewed as routine. And he rejoiced with the other pilots who regularly delivered the mail to the communities along the North

DH 83C Fox Moth
Engine: DH Gipsy III
120 hp
Speed: Max 107 mph (172 KmH)
Speed: Cruise 94 mph (151 KmH)
Ceiling: 14,000 feet (4000 M)
Range: 385 miles (619 KM)
Note: Shorty flew his last jobs for Canadian Airways in August, 1938 in this aircraft (CF-APG)
Canada Aviation Museum Photo ID 1873

Shore of the St. Lawrence when, in 1937, the former Vice President of Quebec Airways, Romeo Vachon, was awarded the McKee Trophy. The trophy, formally known as The Trans-Canada Trophy, had been established in 1926 by an American, J.Dalzeil McKee, to commemorate the first trans Canada seaplane flight in which he had participated earlier that year. It was awarded annually, "for meritorious service in the advancement of aviation in Canada" and in 1937 it recognized the work that had been done along the North Shore. Vachon, who had been the first pilot to fly the mail out to Sept isles and Anticosti Island in 1928, was chosen to receive it.

The company continued to operate on a reduced scale until World War II when many of its people became involved in the British Commonwealth Air Training Plan. Eventually its assets were purchased by Canadian Pacific Airlines and the Flying Goose symbol which had become so familiar throughout Canada in the 1930s was replaced by the variation adopted by Canadian Pacific.

Those last jobs out of Senneterre also marked the end of Shorty's career as a commercial pilot which had started with his retirement from the RCAF in 1929. For the remainder of his flying life and, indeed, his life in aviation, he would be involved in the development and production of aircraft, some of them newly built models of proven machines, others right off the drawing board.

NC 18388
The Barkley-Grow aircraft in which Shorty spent many hours in the autumn of 1938

T8P-1 Barkley-Grow
Two Pratt & Whitney 450 hp
Max Speed: 220 mph (354 KmH)
Cruise Speed: 185 mph (298 KmH)
Ceiling: 24000 feet (6,680 M)
Range: 750 miles (1200 Km)

Hatton Family Photo

Flying Salesman

The silver, all metal, twin-engine machine bearing United States registration lifted off the field at Wayne and for the next two hours flew over the Michigan countryside with Shorty at the controls and an American examiner at his side. The aircraft was a T8P-1 Barkley Grow and, on September 26th, 1938, Shorty was being rated to fly aircraft registered in the United States.

The world was changing rapidly in 1938. Germany, which had been devastated at the end of the war in 1918, had a new charismatic leader in the person of Adolf Hitler, who was bringing the country out of appalling depression primarily through an intense rearmament program. The international community had mixed opinions about him. The Canadian Prime Minister, Mackenzie King, never noted for his understanding of anything other than back room politics, thought he was a "harmless peasant". When Germany had made demands for the return of territory lost in the war, the British Prime Minister, Neville Chamberlain, agreed promising "peace in our time" and assuring the world that, in his view, Hitler had no other territorial ambitions in Europe. More thoughtful people were not so sure. A terrible civil war was raging in Spain and German weapons, even soldiers and pilots, were being tested with great success by the Insurgents under Francisco Franco who, like Hitler, was a Fascist.

In Britain, the armed forces were quietly being brought up to some sort of modern capability following the neglect of the previous twenty years. Even in Canada, the politicians had been persuaded to make some effort to change the Royal Canadian Air Force from a super flying club into a military organization and arrangements had been made to purchase some modern fighter aircraft. Far seeing leaders in Canadian industry were looking ahead and, in one company at least, steps had been taken to prepare for the future.

Canadian Car and Foundry had been founded early in the century as a manufacturer, as its name implied, of railway cars, but in the mid to late thirties changes were being made. It reopened a plant it had closed in Fort William years before, this time to be engaged in the manufacture of aircraft. It also acted as agent and distributor of some US built aircraft from its Montreal office. In 1934 Colonel R.H.Mulock, he who had pulled together the Eastern Division of Canadian Airways, joined the company. In 1937 Victor M. Drury who had been on the Canadian Airways Board of Directors for years became President. His brother, Chipman, another former Canadian Airways officer, also became involved in the company. All of these men, were of course, known to Shorty and he to them. By the summer of 1938 they had been joined by two other Canadian Airways stalwarts and close friends, Murray Semple and Cookie. They introduced him to another company officer, David Boyd, the manager of Canadian Car's aircraft plant at Fort William. In Montreal there were long conversations about the times to come, the possibility of war, the future of aircraft production and the difficulties faced by Canadian Airways without a franchise to run a national airline.

> **Fort William (Thunder Bay)**
> Fort William was established as a fur trading post at the mouth of the Kaminstiquia River on the north shore of Lake Superior in 1803 by the North West Company. In 1870 another community, Port Arthur, emerged some kilometres to the east. It grew rapidly and an intense rivalry developed between the two municipalities. Following completion of the Canadian Pacific Railway in 1885, the area became a major port for the shipment of grain from the prairies and Canadian Car and Foundry built a plant to manufacture rail cars in Fort William. In 1907 both communities became cities and developed similarly but seperately. In 1970 under pressure from the provincial government they were incorporated in the city of Thunder Bay.

In September Shorty was hired by Canadian Car and Foundry as a staff pilot, operating out of Montreal. Initially he was employed flying company owned Stinson Reliants, CF-BGP and CF-BGO, in and about Longeuil to demonstrate them or on charter work, but late in the month he had journeyed to Michigan to be checked out on the American built Barkley Grow.

Canadian Car had acquired the world-wide sales rights outside the USA for this new aircraft which had been designed and built by a small new company in Wayne, Michigan. Archibald S.Barkley and Harold B. Grow, both aviation pioneers in the United States, had joined forces and developed an eight seat twin engine plane which they called the T8P-1 (Transport, 8 place, first model) but which became generally known as the Barkley-Grow. It was a modern all metal machine not unlike the Electras Shorty had flown during his brief period with TCA. Unlike other similar aircraft of the era it did not have retracting wheels and was easily recognized by the unique "wheel pants" or faired landing gear. Barkley Grow had demonstrated the design to the Royal Air Force and, in an expansion effort aimed at finding enough money to develop a newer version (T8P-2) with retractable gear for the RAF, had run into financial problems. To prevent its existing aircraft from being seized by creditors in the United States, the company eventually moved them into Canada where Canadian Car attempted to sell them.

The prototype was initially registered as NX 18388 and first flew in April 1937. When certified it became NC 18388 and Shorty spent most of October,

1938, taking it on a long demonstration tour of Canada from St. Hubert to Ottawa, then across Northern Ontario to Porquis Junction and Wogaming to Fort William. There he spent two days demonstrating the aircraft to officials at the Canadian Car plant and to city dignitaries who were hoping to build a new airport which could become a major stop for Trans Canada Airlines. Then it was off to Winnipeg via Kenora. More local flights in the Winnipeg area were followed by a trip to Regina, Lethbridge, Edmonton for two days, Saskatoon, and back, via Regina, to Winnipeg. On October 26th he made the long flight home to St Hubert via Sioux Lookout, Wogaming, Porquis Junction and Ottawa.

Early in November he flew NC 18388 to the new Toronto area airport at Malton and then to Detroit where he left the aircraft. Early in 1939 three were sold to Yukon Southern Airways for one dollar each and, as they say in the NHL, "future considerations". The deal was negotiated by Yukon's president, Grant McConachie who eventually became president of Canadian Pacific Airlines, after that company had absorbed Yukon in 1941.

On Tuesday, February 28th 1939, after a long period on the ground, Shorty spent about an hour flying locally around St Hubert in CF-BLK, an aircraft that was new to him and quite different from the twin engine passenger plane on which he had spent so much time since leaving Canadian Airways. BLK was formally known as a Grumman G-23, and was one of 52 assembled by Cancar from US built components at the Ft William plant between 1938 and 1940. Much later, when it went into service with the RCAF, it called the Goblin.

It was a fighter plane, a version of the Grumman FF-1 which had been designed in the early 30s and taken into service in the United States Navy for carrier operations in 1933. A biplane, it was rather stubby with a huge engine and wells for retractable landing gear in the belly just ahead of the lower wing. Designed for two people, the pilot and an observer, it had a canopy over the crew compartment. Its maximum speed was 223 miles per hour and a far cry from the military aircraft he had flown ten years before in the RAF and RCAF. But even at that it was not in a class with the newer aircraft that would fight the Second World War - the Spitfires, the Messerschmitts and the Hurricanes. In the United States Navy it had been phased out of service for updated versions which, while similar in appearance, could out-perform it.

There has always been a bit of mystery and, perhaps, scandal about Canadian Car's 1936 decision to build this obsolescent aircraft. At that time Spain was in a messy civil war with international implications. The Insurgents, headed by Francisco Franco were supported by their fellow European fascists ; Hitler in

Germany and Mussolini in Italy. The opposing Republicans or Loyalists were supported by the Communists and, in sympathy at least, by many people in North America who feared the activities of of the Nazis in Germany.

When Cancar first obtained its licence to build the G-23 it was for forty aircraft to be supplied to the Spanish Republicans, however the order was cancelled in keeping with an arms embargo on Spain : an embargo that was honoured in Britain, the United States and Canada but not by the European fascists who continued to supply Franco with arms, aircraft and other support. Shortly after cancelling the Spanish order Cancar received another, this time from Turkey, for forty G-23's. This order was placed by an agent in Paris, one Dr. Katz. No one at Canadian Car or in the government seems to have noticed the amazing coincidence that this same Katz was the fellow who had placed the original order for the Spanish aircraft and production went ahead.

It is interesting to note that the Fort William Times-Journal published a major story on the project in its issue of April 16th, 1938. On the front page, illustrated with two large photographs, much is made of the 22nd aircraft being completed and shipped from the Fort William plant. Conspicuous by its absence is any mention of the location to which the planes were being shipped or any identification of the recipients. But in the United States, the Federal Bureau of Investigation had learned the destination. Shipment of the aircraft, which were essentially of U.S. origin, was contrary to the neutrality laws.

On October 28th, the State Department issued a statement that the order had been a forgery on official government letterhead stolen in Turkey. The shipments from Canada were destined for Istanbul but made "intermediate stopovers" at the French port of Le Havre.The Canadian government started to look a little more closely at the deal and conceded that the FBI might be right. On 11 April, 1938 the freighter " Hada County" sailed from Montreal but was intercepted and forced to return. Her cargo of parts for 16 aircraft was confiscated and returned to Fort William. By the time the bureaucracy caught up the the situation and shipment was halted, seventeen G-23's had been sent to Spain.

Although arrests were made in Turkey over the forged documents, Canadian Car was in the clear. Dave Boyd was away in England at the time but his assistant, E.J.Soulsby, stated that a Turkish agent (or someone posing as one), after paying for them, took possession of the aircraft at the plant.

All of which may have amused Shorty who never failed to find the humour in bureaucratic tangles but was of little immediate consequence to him as he checked himself out on BLK and a week later when he flew her to Ottawa. When

Spanish G-23s

The seventeen aircraft that reached Spain went into action as 28 Group made up of two squadrons. The first operated out of Valencia and took part in the defence of the east coast. The second operated on the Ebro front.

One was damaged when the pilot hit high tension cables during a dive bombing attack. Two others collided after one was struck by antiaircraft artillery. Yet another was hit and landed in enemy territory. Several were bombed and four were captured.

At the end of hostilies the surving aircraft fled to Algiers, whose authoriries handed them over to the victors. These were used by the Spanish Government as a unit based in the Balearic islands and continued in service until about 1955.

the Spanish order had been turned back at St John the company continued to build G-23's. There had been rumours in the press in April, 1938 of huge orders including 105 for an "unnamed South American company" and 45 others "pending". None of these materialized and by the fall of 1938 the company found itself with a number of them on hand. One of them (C/n 143) was registered as CF-BLK to be used as a demonstrator in an effort to sell the machines to the RCAF and on March 8, 1939 Shorty took her to Rockcliffe where Air Force pilots could look her over.

During the visit, a fellow student on the 1933 course at Camp Borden and now an official in the department of Transport, George Wakeman, endorsed his commercial licence to include the Barkley Grow. He stayed in Ottawa for about a week and during that period he demonstrated the aircraft in several flights and at least eleven RCAF officers took her up. They concluded that the aeroplane was too slow and obsolete and declined to buy any. On 29 March he flew her back to Montreal and on the 20th of April he spent about two and half hours in her in the Montreal area.

There was little flying in May except for a brief one day visit in the Stinson, BGP, to Ottawa. Then on June 6th he spent an hour in the Montreal area trying to get comfortable in CF-BMB, the FDB-1 Gregor fighter/dive bomber.

When Canadian Car and Foundry had opened its new aircraft division in the old plant at Fort William in 1937, an engineer of Russian birth and education who had been working in the United States joined the company as Chief Aeronautical Engineer. Michael Gregor was busy designing a new fighter/dive bomber. When he was replaced as Chief Engineer by Elizabeth MacGill in 1938, he stayed on with Cancar to devote all his time to the project.

The result of Gregor's work was a single place biplane which he hoped would reach a top speed, with a suitable engine, of 362 miles per hour. It was stubby little plane with a fat round fuselage and immense engine, vaguely reminiscent of the Grumman G-23s already under construction at the plant. The pilot sat in a canopy cockpit and peered out, with difficulty, according to those who flew it, over the upper wing. It looked more like the aircraft of World War I than the sleek fighters that would win the Battle of Britain in less than two years. One prototype was built and test flown at Fort William by George F.G.Adye on December 17th, 1938. It was subsequently registered as CF-BMB.

In the spring of 1939, BMB had been taken to Montreal for Certificate of Airworthiness tests which were conducted by Flight Lieutenant Lawrence E.Wray, RCAF. While not being too harsh, Wray commented on several weaknesses in his official report, including the fact that the controls were too sensitive and that the flap area or angles should be reduced. He commented on the visibility problem and noted that it had utterly failed to reach up to the designer's expectations by only reaching a top speed of 261 miles per hour.

**FDB-1 Gregor Fighter/Dive Bomber.
CF-BMB**
Airplane Photo Supply Photo #195

Shortly after Wray's tests, on June 6th, Shorty flew the aircraft locally at St Hubert for about an hour and in that flight discovered another of its weaknesses. The cockpit had been designed around the original test pilot, George Adye, a very big man, and Shorty did not appreciate, until he was airborne, just how big Adye was. " I took this thing up and I thought I'd do a slow roll and I got her over on her back, but trying to get the stick forward to complete it, I couldn't reach it - I couldn't get it forward. He could reach about a foot further than I could, so I was up there upside down. All I could do was come back down and I was getting awfully close to the ground so I had to pull back in a hell of a hurry and shoot straight back up in the air again. The first thing I knew I was up to several thousand feet and just coming to."

It was several years before the invention of the "G" suit which would have overcome the intense gravitational forces he experienced and he had blacked out, for the first and only time in his flying career.

A week later, on 12 June, he ferried her to Ottawa where, over the next eight days he conducted several local flights for the RCAF, presumably a repeat performance of his activities in March with the G-23. In view of Flight Lieutenant Wray's report, the fact that the Air Force was about to receive British built Hawker Hurricanes and his own assessment of the Gregor, it is hard to believe that he seriously contemplated a sale.

His formal comments on the aircraft were not recorded at the time but in a 1967 interview with William J. Wheeler, an aircraft writer and illustrator, he too, had words about the Gregor's oversensitivity and too much flap. He suggested that it was not a plane for an inexperienced pilot. Perhaps he was being polite. Gwen well remembers his private comments made at the time he was flying the machine in Montreal. He told her that it was, "the most dangerous aeroplane he had ever been in" and that, "it should not be allowed to fly".

On July 12th he picked up a new Barkley Grow, NC 18469, at Detroit and ferried her to Toronto for a number of demonstration flights before heading back to St Hubert via Ottawa. For the remainder of July his flying was confined to NC 18469 in the Montreal area.

Early in August he took one of the Stinson Reliants, BGO, over to Cornwall and then up to Rouyon area where he had been flying for Canadian Airways the previous summer. These two Reliants, CF-BGO and CF-BGP were operated by Canadian Car as demonstrators for a couple of years, leased to Canadian Airways for a while and then finished their service during the war in the Royal Norwegian Air Force which operated flying schools on Toronto Island and in Muskoka near Bracebridge, Ontario.

Wednesday August 23rd, 1939 was a hot, muggy day in Detroit Michigan. It was sweltering inside the all-metal fuselage of NC 18469, which the company hoped to sell to a wealthy American businessman in the area, but there was no alternative for Gwen other than to sit there for hours and endure it while Shorty struggled with officials of the US Customs and Immigration service. It had looked like a good opportunity to get away for a day or two at company expense but now she was not so sure. Apparently someone had failed to make the necessary border crossing arrangements as promised and they were not expected. Eventually he was able to make contact with Murray Semple back at the Montreal office and in due time the bureaucrats released them and they were able to escape from the steamy runway and register at the hotel.

The following day Shorty flew the machine to Grayling, in Michigan's Upper Peninsula, where he put it through its paces for the customer. Gwen stayed in the hotel, slightly alarmed at this experience of being left alone on her own in a big, strange city, but the next day he picked her up and they returned, via Toronto to Montreal. For the little girls at home, they had wonderful presents. Each of them received little black dolls " all dressed in white dimity dresses with little red spots on them" that Gwen had been able to buy in Detroit. In those days people of African descent were a rarity in most parts of Canada and these unusual, for Canadian children, gifts were treasured by the girls for years. Sue, who was only four at the time, still remembers hers with fondness.

A week later, on September 1st, 1939, in spite of promises made to the British Prime Minister, Neville Chamberlain, Hitler's German troops invaded Poland and, on the 3rd, Britain declared war on Germany. In Canada there was formal hesitation to enter this European war and in Ottawa the politicians pondered the situation. No such doubts bothered the minds of many Canadians, particularly those with military experience or in the defence related industries. By the time Parliament formally declared war a week later, military mobilization plans had been implemented and many companies, including Canadian Car, were actively working on their plans to get into wartime production.

On September 10th while the Members of Parliament were solemnly committing Canada to the Second World War, Shorty was just a couple of miles down the Ottawa River at Rockcliffe delivering NC 18469 to the RCAF. After two days of conducting familiarization flights with RCAF pilots he formally handed it over and it became RCAF 758 assigned to 12 Squadron. It only served the air force for a year and then was sold to Maritime Central Airways as CF-BMV. It was destroyed in 1942 during an attempt to rescue the crew of a downed USAAF B-17 in Greenland.

Those flights at Rockcliffe were to be his last in the Barkley Grow. All told only eleven were ever produced and seven of them were known to have been purchased in Canada. Mackenzie Air Service operated two of them for a number of years, one went to Peru and another was used by Admiral Byrd on his 1939 Antarctic expedition. NC 18388, the prototype and the one in which Shorty conducted a cross Canada tour in 1938 was eventually sold to Prairie Airways in Moose Jaw, Saskatchewan and registered as CF-BVE. It is on display in the Reynolds-Alberta Museum in Wetaskiwan, Alberta. One of three Yukon Southern Airways machines, CF-BLV, is now in the Aerospace Museum at Calgary, Alberta bearing Canadian Pacific markings.

In late September Shorty went to Fort William where he tested two of the newly built G-23's (C/n's 144 and 145) as they came off the production line. He was to meet these aircraft again but now his career as a test pilot took an abrupt turn. Immediately after completing the tests on G-23 C/n 145 on 30 September he was sent to England to be checked out on a vastly superior fighter: the Hawker Hurricane.

The First of Many
P5170, the first Hawker Hurricane built by Candian Car and Foundry at Fort William, Ontario. Test flown by Shorty Hatton 0n 10 January, 1940.

Photo Courtesy Canada Aviation Museum

Test Pilot

On a cold, crisp day early in the new year of 1940, Shorty climbed into a sleek, modern fighter aircraft at Bishop's Field in Fort William and, after carefully checking everything, ran up the powerful Rolls-Royce Merlin III engine and roared off into the Northern Ontario sky. For thirty minutes he crossed and circled over the heavy bush that grew almost to the edge of the airfield and then, satisfied, brought this wonderful aeroplane back to earth. It was January 10th and the plane was P5170, a Hawker Hurricane Mark I ; the first of 1,451 that would be built in Canada over the next four years.

The Hawker Hurricane had been designed in 1934 by Sydney Cramm who journeyed to Fort William to witness this first Canadian flight. It was developed in Great Britain by Hawker Aircraft Limited and first flown on 6 November, 1936 by George Bulman. It went into squadron service in the Royal Air Force late in 1937. A low wing monoplane, it was initially fitted with a Rolls Royce Merlin engine that gave speeds well in excess of 300 miles per hour, and was, in its day, one of the hottest flying machines in the world. As they were produced for the RAF, and as it became increasingly apparent that war in the near future was a distinct possibility, the Royal Canadian Air Force made arrangements to purchase some from Britain.

At about the same time, in November 1938, Canadian Car and Foundry received a contract to build 40 of them at the Fort William plant but when the war started in September 1939, while some had been delivered from Britain to the RCAF, none had been produced in Canada. The start of the war gave added impetus to the project.

In October 1939 Shorty had sailed for England after a grand farewell party at the Windsor Hotel in Montreal thrown by Dave Boyd, who, as plant manager at Fort William, was responsible for the Hurricane project. The ocean liners, many of which he had flown out to meet at Rimouski in days gone by, were still operating on their peace time schedules. That would change within weeks to carry the Canadian Army's 1st Division to Britain, but the great convoys out of Halifax were yet to be formed and it was essentially as a peace time passenger that he leaned on the rail and watched the pilot being dropped at Father Point, where just a few years before, he had picked up the mail from overseas. Then the ship made her lonely dash across the Atlantic.

Gwen's sister, Dougie, had come down from Ontario for the affair at the Windsor and, during the emotional farewells, grew quite weepy and invited Gwen and the girls to come and stay with them during Shorty's absence. Bob Denman's financial fortunes continued to soar and he had recently purchased a fairly extensive property in a small village, Greensville, near Hamilton. In addition to a large old imposing, stone main house there were several other buildings including a complete farm house which was occupied by a hired man and his family and a smaller dwelling which would, in a later, time probably be described as a Granny Flat. It had a fairly large living room, bedroom, kitchen and adequate bathroom and was only a few hundred yards from the main house. It proved to be the ideal temporary residence for Gwen and the girls while Shorty was away. Although the prospect of Christmas apart was not pleasant there was the knowledge that thousands of Canadian families were in the same boat.

There was also a difficult mix-up with Shorty's pay and Gwen found herself in Ontario with, to her dismay, no money. It took several telephone calls to the company in Montreal to straighten it out. There was some slight compensation. For the first time in years the Glassco girls could be together. Dougie was of course, next door. Ann and her family also lived in Greensville, less than a mile away and Margie and their parents were just a half hour's drive off in Hamilton. Joyce, now eight years old, was enrolled in the local school with her cousins. Still it was a difficult winter.

While they were able to celebrate that first wartime Christmas in some sort of family atmosphere, Shorty was not so lucky. He had a very short time in which to visit the Hawker Siddley factory and other facilities to learn everything he needed to know to fly and to test the Hurricane. It was his first visit back to England since leaving eleven years before but there was little time for socializing. At one point early in his visit he was in the bar of the Royal Air Force Club in London with an associate from Hawker Siddley who turned to him and casually asked , "Do you have a brother who lives in England ?"

Shorty acknowledged that he did and his companion remarked, "Well he's sitting right down at the end of the bar".

Shorty sauntered down and, as though they had parted the day before, simply said, "Hi Bill".

It was not hard to understand how the colleague had recognized his brother. At first glance a stranger might assume them to be twins, so alike were they in appearance, voice and manner. After about 15 years in India where he had married the daughter of a British doctor and fathered a family, Bill had returned to England. Now with a war on he was in the Royal Air Force doing an administrative job. The brothers were able to arrange other meetings and Shorty managed to get enough time off from work to spend a few days with Bill and his family at their home in Devon. Bill also persuaded him to patch up the rift with his father that had kept them apart since the failure of his parent's marriage so many years before and he travelled down to visit the old gentleman.

On November 28th he flew his first Hurricane, N2527, at the Hawker Aircraft Ltd.. production and experimental factory at Langley in Buckinghamshire, just west of London. A week later, after logging only a little more than two hours in the machine but considerably more in the factory, he was certified as an Air Ministry Acceptance Pilot. Then it was time to head back to Fort William and, just before Christmas, Bill took him to the station to see him off on the boat train. Bill asked an attendant if it would be possible to delay the train's departure for just a few minutes. His brother was leaving for Canada, he explained, and they wanted to have a last drink together because, "We'll probably never see each other again".

He was right. They never did.

Shorty spent that Christmas on the Atlantic Ocean. Although he never knew exactly where they were on the high seas, one thing was certain. As the weather grew almost tropical it became obvious that the ship was veering a long way south to avoid the enemy submarines that were already lurking in the North Atlantic. On arrival in Halifax he went immediately to Fort William arriving just as the first Hurricane, P5170, was ready to fly.

On being accepted as a test pilot Shorty had achieved a designation accorded to very few flyers. At that time there were 1,300 licensed pilots in Canada but only eight of them were accepted by the insurance underwriters as test pilots. The approval of the insurance industry was vital to designers and manufacturers of aircraft who, naturally, wished to protect their investment in the aircraft. This they did with three types of insurance; "ground risk', "hull risk" , i.e. flight insurance and public liability, should something happen during testing that might injure a member of the public or damage private property. Before a company would issue a policy it would conduct a thorough investigation into the test pilot's record and qualifications.In that winter of 1940 the pilots, "known to the underwriters" and actively testing aircraft were in addition to Shorty:

- Dick Bibby, who was now working for Vickers,
- Leigh Capreol, at National Steel Car and Ottawa Car and Aircraft Co., testing Westland Lysanders,
- Red Lymburner, a fellow student on the Canadian Airways 1936 Instrument Flying Course, testing Bristol Bolingbrokes for Fairchild Aircraft in

Montreal,

- George R. Spadbrow who was soon to fly the de Havilland DH 89 Mosquito prototype.

Three others who were recognized but not actively testing at the time were George Adye, who had tested the Gregor, Jack Sanderson and Jimmie Town.

Amidst the glamour generated by public relations people and the film industry, it is easy to lose sight of the everyday work of the test pilot. While much is made of the dangerous, often quite short, time the pilot spends in the air, his other duties are often overlooked. In an interview with writer Ted Mosher for the March 1940 issue of Canadian Aviation magazine, Leigh Capreol broke the job down into four components:

1. Careful and continuous study of the aircraft in question during development and production

2. The ability to notice small details which call for correction

3. The ability to analyse flying performance and suggest changes that will put it right

4. The ability to fly with utmost precision, while at the same time making notes for the test report.

A few years later, J.H.Orrell, A.V.Roe's Chief Test Pilot on the Avro Manchester Airliner expressed his thoughts on the qualities of a test pilot. " He now needs to be an engineer and a pilot, with inquisitive mind and the ability to analyse the value of an aircraft, its controls, power plant and equipment with concise accuracy to assist the designer and experimental department."

None of the Canadian test pilots in the early 40s were graduate engineers but the successful ones met Orrell's other criteria and worked very closely with the engineers. There is a special relationship between the aeronautical engineers who build aircraft and the test pilots who risk their lives seeing if the ideas work. They learn from each other as they discover problems, discuss them at length and solve them. At Canadian Car Shorty had the privilege of working with a brilliant aeronautical engineer, Elizabeth MacGill.

One of the men who worked with her at Fort William remembered that she ran the engineering department with an iron fist. He described her by saying that, "If you wanted to say 'Good Morning', she was likely to snap back, 'If I wanted a weather report I would have phoned the airport'".

In time her unusual work was highlighted in a comic book published during the war to convince young Canadians raised on tales of British and American heroes that we had our own.

> **Elizabeth "Elsie" Muriel Gregory MacGill**
>
> Elsie MacGill was born in Vancouver, BC in 1905. She attended the University of Toronto where, in 1927, she became the first woman in Canada to earn a degree in electrical engineering. She entered the University of Michigan for graduate work but contracted "infantile paralysis" (polio) in the final weeks of her work there. In spite of her acute pain she finished her course in 1929 and became the only woman in the world to hold a Master's degree in aeronautical engineering.
>
> Although initially confined to a wheelchair, she struggled with her paralysis, eventually managing to walk using canes. When she recovered enough she enrolled for further studies at the Massachusetts Institute of Technology in Boston. That led to employment with Fairchild Aircraft Ltd. in Montreal where she worked on the design of aircraft and the testing of wind tunnels. In 1938 she became the first woman elected to the Engineering Institute of Canada.
>
> Acting as her company's representative during testing at the National Research Council of Canada's new world standard wind tunnels in Ottawa and as passenger on all test flights she quickly earned a profile in her industry. These activities led to her election as the first woman corporate member of the Engineering Institute of Canada in 1938 and a new job as Chief Aeronautical Engineer at the Canadian Car and Foundry aircraft plant at Fort William Ontario. There she worked on the development of a training aircraft, The Maple Leaf, which, although it gained its certificate of airworthiness was never produced in quantity. She was chief engineer for most of the production of Hawker Hurricanes but then left with her husband for Toronto where she established herself as a consultant
>
> In 1953 she was named "Woman Engineer of the Year" by the American Society of Women Engineers and in 1971 made a member of the Order of Canada. She is a member of the Canadian Science and Engineering Hall of fame and the Canadian Aviation Hall of Fame. Although she never did fly a plane the International Association of Women Pilots awarded her the Amelia Earhart Medal. She died in 1980.

It was more than a month after that first test, before the next Hurricane, P5171, was ready and during the period, Shorty was able to spend a couple of hours flying P5170 before it was on its way to join one of the twenty-six RAF squadrons that were to be equipped in Britain before the massive attacks in the late summer.

He was also sent briefly back to St Hubert for a bit more time in the Gregor. It had been entered in an international air race in January but a problem with oil pressure forced it out. After considerable work on the machine in Montreal, Shorty spent about an hour and a half on February 14th giving it a thorough test following which it was placed in storage where it was burnt in a 1945 fire. The FDB-1 Gregor was the first fighter aircraft designed in Canada and CF-

BMB was the only one built.

After testing the second Hurricane on February 28th, another nine days passed before the third was ready and during the period he conducted a number of tests on one of the RCAF Mark II machines. By then a routine had developed based on the system in use at Langley. On the ground he would carefully check the engine, hydraulics and brakes and then take off and climb to 14,000 feet, recording engine figures and trims at 4,000 foot intervals. At 14,000 he would fly straight and level for two minutes at full power to record maximum speed. Then a sharp dive, during which he would reach 400 miles per hour to 8,000 feet to check trims. Another dive to 5,000 feet for stall tests with flap and undercarriage up and down and then back to the airport where any necessary adjustments were made to the aircraft. There was usually a second test after the adjustments were completed and then the aircraft was signed off as ready for shipment.

For the next few months he tested more and more in this way and accepted them on behalf of the British Air Ministry: four in March, four more in April, six in May and eight more in June. All of them were dispatched immediately to the RAF which was to desperately need them before the summer ended.

On July 10th, Hitler launched the first phase of what would be known as The Battle of Britain. For the next month, until mid-August, the Luftwaffe launched daily raids on shipping in the English Channel and on the dock facilities in Southern England. Phase two started on 13 August with all raids aimed at the RAF fields and facilities in England.

In Fort William, Canadian Car under Dave Boyd's leadership, was rapidly expanding from an initial work force of 610 to 3,500. They heard the daily newscasts from London on the BBC Overseas service which was carried on the new Canadian radio network. The tolling of Big Ben followed by the solemn English voice informing the world that two or three of our aircraft had been destroyed was a daily reminder to increase production. Even more of an incentive was the news that the German losses to RAF Hurricanes were greater and the number of completed machines continued to grow. On the 29th of July Shorty tested and accepted the 39th, P5208. Just one month later, on August 31st, it was shot down while serving in No. 601 Squadron RAF; the first Canadian built Hawker Hurricane to be lost in action.

Hurricanes, Goblins and Helldivers

In May 1940, with Hurricane production and testing well under way at Fort William, the war had taken a nasty turn in Europe. Germany invaded France, Belgium and the Netherlands. The Allied forces on the continent were reeling from the Blitzkrieg as German armour, closely supported by the Luftwaffe, rolled over the badly equipped French and British armies. In June, France collapsed and the remnants of the British Army were evacuated at Dunkirk. It had become a different war and in Canada authorities were, for the first time since the Fenian raids of the late 1800s, thinking seriously about defending Canadian soil.

Given our post-war knowledge of German capabilities in 1940, it is difficult to imagine the threat to Canada's east coast that seemed to bother the authorities in Ottawa. As it turned out, the Royal Air Force was able to defeat the Luftwaffe in the Battle of Britain later that year and the Germans found it prudent to cancel any plans they had for the invasion of England. Nevertheless, a direct threat to Canada was perceived and there were no fighter planes at all on the East Coast to meet it. When Canadian Car reminded the RCAF that there were a number of G-23's sitting in a shed at Fort William, the Air Force thought that they might not be so obsolete after all and agreed to buy them. One can only imagine the glee in the Canadian Car and Foundry board room at the prospect of unloading these white elephants.

At Fort William the G-23s were quickly finished to RCAF specifications and on Friday, August 9th, Shorty broke off testing Hurricanes and started an intensive seven week period of testing them. At first he spent a number of hours

> **The Battle of Britain**
> In the spring of 1940, German troops occupied most of continental Europe and the Nazi leader, Adolph Hitler set his sights on the conquest of Great Britain. The German air force (Luftwaffe) started major air raids on the country to establish air superiority before launching an attack across the English Channel. The defeat of the air attacks has become known as The Battle of Britain. There is some controversy about the actual dates of the battle but it is safe to say that it took place between 1 July and 31 October, 1940. At the time the German raids started the Royal Air Force had 347 operational Hawker Hurricanes in 29 squadrons and 199 Supermarine Spitfires in 19 squadrons. In that late summer and early autumn the RAF fighters prevented the Germans from destroying the radar installations and the fighter command airfields. German raids on the population of London proved even less successful merely serving to strengthen the resolve of the people. The British lost 930 aircraft while the Germans lost 1623. Hitler abandoned all ideas of invading Britain. Prime Minister Winston Churchill was able to salute the Hurricane and Spitfire pilots, "Never in the world of human conflict has so much been owed by so many to so few".

in C/n 145, the aircraft he had initially tested just before going to England almost a year before. On a number of flights he carried RCAF officers as observers and on Friday August 16th with J.J."Joe" Russell, Canadian Car's Chief Inspector, on board he took her up to 27 thousand feet to test the heaters which he found to be satisfactory. Then the testing fell into a routine: Shorty would fly each aircraft solo for about 30 minutes and then for about an hour with an RCAF observer on board. On Thursday 10 October, 1940 he tested his last G-23. It was one of the earlier ones manufactured originally for Turkey/Spain (C/n 142) and was accepted by the Air Force and placed into service as RCAF 339. The RCAF formally called the aircraft the Goblin, but many of the airmen referred it as the "Pregnant Frog".

 # 118 Squadron (Fighter) Royal Canadian Air Force
G-23 Grumman Goblins (Pregnant Frogs)
Shorty Hatton tested each of these planes before they were delivered to the RCAF, Autumn 1941

RCAF Photo

By December all fifteen Goblins were operational in the newly formed No. 118 Squadron (Fighter) at RCAF Station Rockcliffe. In July 1941 the squadron moved to Dartmouth, Nova Scotia and about five months later received Curtis Kittyhawk fighters from the United States. The Goblins were then taken out of service and, by the Spring of 1942, all of them had been scrapped. Those that had made it through the embargo to Spain fought against the superior Fascist aircraft and only eight of them survived the Spanish Civil War. They were taken into service in the Spanish Air Force and the last one was scrapped in 1955. But one of the fifty-two G-23's built by Canadian Car & Foundry survived. Interestingly enough, it was the first one built (C/n 101) and test flown on February 3rd, 1938. It was sold to Nicaragua and ended up in a scrap yard. Later it was purchased by an American aviation enthusiast who rebuilt it and sent it to the U.S. Naval Aviation Museum at Pensacola. It is shown in US Navy colours in an illustration in the

Grumman Corporation's history book, "Grumman - Sixty years of Excellence" by Bill Gunston.

By the time the Nazis admitted, at least to themselves, that they could not achieve air superiority over Britain and abandoned their plans to invade in late September, Shorty had accepted over fifty Canadian Car Hurricanes and seen them on their way. And production continued at an ever increasing rate.

When the first Hurricanes were built they had been equipped with engines manufactured in Britain, but as time went on it was realized that this two-way flow of engines across the Atlantic was not necessary. Many were then shipped, untested, without engines for final acceptance in Britain. However a number of engines were held at Fort William and periodically Shorty would designate an aircraft on the production line for testing. After it had been fitted with an engine he would check it out in the air before it went on its way. His first test on this system took place on September 28th when he broke off testing G23s long enough to fly a MK I machine, T9519.

Early in 1941 production shifted to the MK X version of the Hurricane in which the Rolls Royce Merlin was replaced with a Packard Merlin 28 engine. The first was ready for testing on March 4th and on that day Shorty conducted an extended hour and a half test of AE 962.

In the spring of 1941 fifty machines purchased by the RCAF were fitted as MK XIIA Sea Hurricanes with a slightly more powerful Packard 29 engine and eight guns. Shorty tested the first of these, (BW 835) on July 4th and later that month ferried her on a four and a half hour flight to to North Bay. The following day, July 25th, he made the relatively short one hour flight to Ottawa and delivered her to the new owners.

By the summer of 1941, there were enough planes in service for the government to feel that at least one could be diverted for public relations purposes and it was decided to display a Cancar Hurricane at the Canadian National Exhibition in Toronto. In August Shorty ferried the newly built AG 325 to Toronto with stops en route to refuel. At that time, six months before the United States was to enter the war, Hollywood was doing its bit by making a film about the British Commonwealth Air Training Plan. Jimmy Cagney was the star and he played the part of an experienced Canadian bush pilot who spent more time fist fighting than flying and had all sorts of implausible adventures before becoming involved in the BCATP and running afoul of RCAF discipline. The movie was made at several RCAF stations and on location in Northern Ontario where the film company had gathered a number of civilian Fairchilds and other bush planes of the era which were handled by local operators. These people became quite excited when Shorty filed his flight plan including a refuelling stop at their location. There was much chatter about the impending arrival of a "Hurricane". The Hollywood people, perhaps unaware of Northern Ontario weather patterns or the reputation of the Hawker aeroplane, immediately postponed filming and ordered all company leased aircraft tied down ! According to Shorty, they were still waiting for the high winds when he and AG 325 were safely on the ground in Toronto. The Hurricane was duly displayed in the Automotive Building at "the Ex" in a rope enclosure which kept small starry-eyed boys from touching it with their grubby hands. After the Exhibition Shorty flew it back to Fort William and in due time it went into Canadian service as RCAF 1359.

As the months went by there were other variations in the basic Hurricanes being produced at Fort William. The MK IIB had a Rolls Royce Merlin engine but the wings were modified to hold twelve .303 Browning machine guns and bomb racks. The MK IIC had four 20mm Oerlikon guns in the wings along with the bomb racks. The MK XII, which was the version favoured by the RCAF, had Packard Merlin Engines and twelve Browning guns.

It was during this summer of 1941 that the Canadian Car plant at Fort William underwent some changes which saw Shorty assuming more responsibility on the ground. The staff had grown to about six thousand, mostly men, but many of those were rapidly being replaced by women who eventually made up 50% of the workers. Much of the credit for the rapid and successful expansion of the operation was due to the remarkable leadership of the General Manager, Dave Boyd. Under his guiding hand production was now up to nine or ten finished aircraft each week. Boyd was a McGill educated engineer who had joined the company when it first went into the aircraft business. He was a shirt sleeves engineer who spent a lot of time on the shop floor, encouraging the workers or handing out rockets when they were needed. He was also comfortable in the executive offices but his greatest asset was his ability to recognize nonsense and cut through it to get the job done. His success at Fort William did not go unnoticed and in that summer of 1941 he was hired away by National Steel Car at Malton, Ontario to sort out the mess that had developed in its aircraft production. At Malton he was largely responsible for the creation of the crown corporation, Victory Aircraft, in which he repeated his Hurricane successes with the production of Lancaster bombers.

Joe Russell, the Chief Inspector at Fort William, was promoted to replace Boyd as General Manager. Elsie MacGill continued on as Chief Engineer and supported the decision to have Shorty appointed to take on Russell's duties as Chief

Inspector. At the same time he retained his appointment as Air Ministry Acceptance Officer for the Hurricanes. He had always been fascinated by mechanical things and Gwen remembers that his idea of a good time at a party was to get in the corner with Elsie MacGill or some other engineer and talk about such esoteric things as horsepower and drag coefficients. All the children recall his attempts to to impress upon them the infinite detail of the inner workings of rotary engines and why they were better (or was it worse?) than the other kind. In his daily dealings with the staff at the plant he was able to add immeasurably to his knowledge. Shorty's new experiences on the production of Hurricanes, coupled with those difficult years in the bush when a pilot, sometimes with his mechanic, sometimes on his own had to repair aircraft engines and other components, now paid off. In spite of no formal schooling in aeronautical design he had, over the years, developed a deep understanding of aircraft construction and engines. Now in his mid-forties it made sense to look to the future on the ground but for the moment, with a war on, there was not much reduction in his flying duties. In 1942 production of the various models reached a peak. Seven hundred were completed and Shorty logged 276 hours in them.

Two that were tested in 1941 held a very special significance for the workers at Canadian Car and the people of Fort William. They were paid for by the workers who worked on two Sundays without pay and were named after two local men who had been killed in the war: Pilot Officer Gary Madore, RAF and Sergeant John Philip Taylor, RCAF.

Madore, who had learned to fly at the Fort William Flying Club had, like a surprisingly large number of Canadians, made his own way to Britain before the start of the Second World War and joined the Royal Air Force. In the spring of 1940 he had been serving at Church Fenton, England in an RAF Hurricane squadron, No. 242. Just after the start of the German offensive, the squadron went into action as described by a brother officer, "On May 23rd the squadron was ordered to escort a reconnaissance aircraft to Cambrai, France from England. Weather conditions were very bad and near Oisy our eleven machines were suddenly attacked by about fifty enemy aircraft. The resulting fight was very confusing".

So confusing that it was not until the squadron returned home that Madore was missed. At first he was listed "Missing" and later "Missing-Presumed Dead". It was not until after the war that his family learned his fate. French eye-witnesses explained that his Hurricane had hit the ground at high speed and he was killed instantly. He is buried in the Commonwealth Military Cemetery at Sailly-sur-Lys in France.

John Taylor had joined the RCAF in 1940 after working at the Canadian Car Plant. After training as a Wireless Air Gunner he had been promoted to Sergeant and sent to England where he continued training on bombers. He was killed early in June, 1941 in a flying accident.

The Hawker-Siddley Chief Test Pilot, George Bulman, who had flown the Hurricane prototype in November, 1935, was visiting from England at the time these two very special planes were dedicated. On Saturday, 19 August, 1941, he and Shorty took them up and proceeded to show the factory workers and their fellow citizens of Fort William just what the Hawker Hurricane could do in the hands of skilled pilots.

Wartime life in Fort William, as in most other Canadian towns and cities fell into a pattern. The favourite expression was, "There's a war on", and it was used to cover every shortage, problem or inadequacy. While unemployment was an unknown word, there were not too many luxuries on which to spend the extra cash that came from war work. Every family member had a food ration book and shopping consisted of budgeting not only the money, but the ration stamps as well. In truth it was not a particularly difficult task for women like Gwen who had learned all about resourceful cooking during the lean years before the war. The spirit of saving was strong and at school, even young Sue at the age of seven or eight was busy saving tinfoil and buying 25 cent War Savings Stamps with her allowance.

Ontario, in those days, while not dry, had the most peculiar liquor regulations. There were establishments called beer parlours in which it was possible to obtain a small glass of draught beer for 10 cents. Most were for men only, although there were others, Ladies Beverage Rooms, where a man could take a female companion, but from which unaccompanied males were banned. Music in these rigidly controlled establishments was forbidden as was almost any other indication of joy. While some hotel dining rooms were permitted to serve a glass of wine with a meal, liquor was not available by the glass anywhere in public. At least, not legally. It could be obtained, by the bottle, from Government Liquor Stores, provided the buyer had a permit in which each purchase was carefully recorded. And the limit was small. In some families ancient and youthful teetotal relatives were frequently persuaded to have their own permits for use by less abstemious family members. Many a young employee at the Canadian Car plant found herself the owner of a liquor permit even though the strongest beverage she might have enjoyed was Coca-Cola. Bootlegging once again became a viable profession.

As a result of all this regulation maintained in the curious theory that it somehow helped defeat the Nazis, the best parties were at home where the order of the day was BYOB (bring your own bottle). Social life centred around the company and, as ever, the people in the aircraft business such as Dave Boyd, Joe Russell and Cookie, who had also moved to Fort William where he was working as a buyer for Canadian Car. Then too, there was another source of social activity for those involved in aviation. There was a Royal Canadian Air Force training station on the airport and mess parties were common.

During the summer of 1940 the forces had expanded in Canada to the point where no self-respecting city or town was without some sort of military establishment. Old buildings in prairie towns were taken over by the Navy, designated "His Majesty's Canadian Ship" and used to train young sailors. The Army purchased land, erected plywood and tar paper shacks, paved a parade square and set about turning civilians into soldiers. A bit farther out of town the Air Force created hangars and laid out runways on what had been farm land. Each was a self-contained community with most of the amenities needed to make life reasonable for the staff and the young people undergoing training: sports facilities, theatres, canteens and messes. Fort William was no exception and the local RCAF establishment, No. 2 Elementary Flying School, was, as in a number of other communities, part of the British Commonwealth Air Training Plan. It operated from the Fort William Municipal Airport to which Canadian Car had moved its flight facilities when Bishop's Field was closed in May, 1940. As an accredited officer of the Air Ministry, to say nothing of his status as a retired officer, Shorty was welcomed as a matter of routine in the officer's mess and he and Gwen frequently attended functions in it. Gwen was amused to find a different sort of Englishman than the one she had married and the others she had known so well in their early married life in St Lambert. A senior officer of the Royal Air Force stationed at the school, thinking perhaps that he had found kindred souls, rather pompously confided to them that he found Fort William to be a dreadful town because his wife could not find, "the right sort of gown in the shops". Gwen found him pretentious. Shorty, who recognized the type, remained polite but unimpressed.

Family life in Fort William was good. On October 15th, 1942 a new member of the family arrived in the person of Ian Malcolm, their youngest child and only son. The girls were growing and were in school. There were very few long trips away from home and the reasonably regular working hours ensured that Shorty could be at home to see them grow and to take part in all of those domestic activities that make family life worth while.

Joyce clearly remembers the Christmas when, with true dedication to the old virtues, Shorty announced that the family would cut its own Christmas tree. Bundled up against the bitter cold and in spite of the need to conserve rationed gasoline, they climbed into the family car and ventured forth to the countryside. There, axe in hand, Shorty trudged off the road into the deep snow. After some searching he found the perfect tree, cut it down and dragged it back to the car. Then, while the women shivered in the minus 40 weather, with the meticulous attention to detail that characterized all of his work, he carefully tied the tree to the car, using a considerable amount of rope, just to be sure. So much rope in fact that when he attempted to get in and drive off he discovered that he had roped himself out the car. That, we are told, was the last year for that sort of expedition. Future Hatton family Christmases would be a boon to the sellers of ready-cut Christmas trees.

One of Shorty's mild passions over the years had been the appreciation of certain foods, primarily those advocated in Mrs Beaton's Cook Book. He established a family wide reputation for his spiced beef which he ritually prepared periodically using home grown herbs.In Fort William he was able get serious about gardening. In those wartime days, Canadians were encouraged to cultivate a "Victory Garden", in which vegetables could be grown for family consumption and Shorty became an enthusiastic gardener. As a result he was able to indulge himself in his enjoyment of pickled onions. Pickled, in season, by Gwen in the kitchen at home and stored for future consumption.

To their delight they found kindred pickled onion souls in the persons of three RAF fighter pilots who had survived the Battle of Britain and had come to Canada to visit the Hurricane plant and incidentally get a bit of a break. From time to time during their stay in Fort William Gwen and Shorty entertained them at home to the delight of Joyce who, on the verge of adolescence, was fascinated by these real life heroes, only a few years older than she. They mentioned that the thing they missed most in wartime England was vegetables and Gwen's store of pickled onions would be reduced dramatically when they came by the house to visit. Eventually the time came for them to depart and the three took off in Hurricanes for delivery to the east Coast, each equipped with a jar of the beloved pickled onions. A couple of days after their departure, Shorty came home with a glum look on his face and said to Gwen, "Well, your pickled onions are at the bottom of the Bay of Fundy".

One of them had gone astray in weather on the coast and had been forced to crash land in the Bay. He sank with his Hurricane before rescue boats could reach him.

There was other depressing news in those wartime days. Bill Drury, who had courted Peg Graham at the Hatton's home in St. Lambert so many years before, had gone into the RCAF and was serving on the east coast. At home on leave he contacted measles from the children but, viewing it as a childhood disease, went back to work flying the long Coastal Command anti-submarine flights out over the Atlantic. He developed pneumonia and died from it in Dartmouth, Nova Scotia on January 17th, 1942.

Other old friends and acquaintances were involved in the war in different ways. Tom Cowley, the professional air force officer, had been promoted and was an Air Vice Marshall serving on the staff in Ottawa. Shorty's old company, Canadian Airways, which was absorbed by Canadian Pacific Airlines in 1941, was involved in the British Commonwealth Air Training Plan. The company had a contract to operate a number of Air Observer Schools for the BCATP and Dick Bibby was the General Manager of # 10 AOS at Chatham, New Brunswick, while Babe Woollett managed # 1 AOS at Malton, Ontario.

In 1943 Shorty logged 112 hours in the air as another 164 Hurricanes of various models were produced at Fort William to bring the total to 1,451 before production was halted in June. By that time they were serving around the world; in Britain, India, Russia, the Middle East and at home in Canadian defence squadrons. Some of the Sea Hurricanes were operated by the Royal Navy's Fleet Air Arm and others were positioned on merchant ships from which they could be catapulted to engage enemy aircraft. And then, most of them just disappeared.

One that was preserved and restored to flying condition by the Canadian Warplane Heritage Museum in Hamilton, Ontario was destroyed in a fire in 1991. Another, RCAF 5584, a Mk XII which was built in November, 1942, is in the National Aviation Museum in Ottawa. Z7015, a Mk I Hurricane, which Shorty flew on January 18th, 1941 is in the Shuttleworth aircraft collection in England. It has been restored to airworthiness and was successfully flown at Duxford, England on September 15th, 1995. Another Fort William Hurricane can still be seen in a film that has become something of a classic. After the war, Robert Diemert of Carman, Manitoba purchased RCAF 5545 and made it airworthy. In due time it was taken to Britain, where in appropriate colours, it was one of the aircraft flown for the movie, "Battle of Britain". It is held in the Strathallan collection in Scotland where it is registered as G-AWLW. A Canadian prairie farmer, Harry Whereatt and his wife Ann, have a MK XII (RCAF 5447) that is close to flying condition as part of their aircraft collection in Assiniboia, Saskatchewan.

The end of Hurricane production did not mean the end of war work at the Canadian Car and Foundry plant at Fort William, but it did reduce Shorty's flying commitments even further and there were other changes. Elsie MacGill had married the Assistant Plant Manager, E.J.Saulsby, who was tempted away from Canadian Car by Dave Boyd to work on the production of Lancasters. Elsie accompanied him to Toronto where she established a consulting firm and settled down to the domestic life.

In May 1942 the Company had received a contract to produce 1,000 Curtis Helldivers. Officially designated the SBW it was a two place low wing monoplane dive bomber initially developed for the U.S.Navy. Others were to be built by Fairchild at Montreal, but the first Canadian Helldiver was ready at Fort William on 22 July 1943 and was tested by Orville J. Weiben who, before joining Cancar, had been the instructor at the Fort William Flying Club.

Helldiver Production
Photo Courtesy Canada Aviation Museum

Shorty's flying did not end completely and over the next couple of years he continued to log air time in a number of different aircraft but for the duration of the war his main duties were on the ground, He supervised the 350 members of the inspection department checking out the 800 or more Helldivers that were built before the contract was cancelled on VJ Day, 14 August 1945.

But before that momentous occasion, there had been another change in his life. By the summer of 1945, the family was back in Montreal and Shorty was back in the cockpit.

Flying Wing

At Cartierville airport on Montreal Island on Friday, July 19th, 1945 Clyde Pangborne of the Burnelli Aircraft Corporation in the United States with Shorty in the right hand seat, eased back on the controls of a strange looking twin engine aircraft and flew. They stayed aloft for an hour and fifty-five minutes and Shorty was able to enter in his log book, "Prototype Test. 1st Flight Burnelli 'Flying Wing'". He was not alone in referring to it by that name but, while it embodied the same principles as some true flying wing aircraft that have come into existence, the description was not entirely accurate.

CF-BEL
Burnelli CBY-3
From an original black and white wash painting by R.W.Bradford for Avro News, 1952.
With Permission

Vincent Burnelli was an American designer who, starting in 1922, had promoted an unusual design which featured a widened fuselage built in an airfoil to provide additional lift as well as increased cabin volume for cargo. His first plane, the American Remington-Burnelli lifting body RB-2, a biplane with an enclosed cabin flew in 1922 but never went into production. Others followed over the years and some of them went into service. When Canadian Car & Foundry first entered the aeroplane business in 1936, it did so with the intention of manufacturing a cargo plane called the Burnelli UB-14 lifting fuselage monoplane which had been successfully test flown in the United States in the summer of '36. A twin engine all metal aircraft designed for passenger, mail and express service it could carry a 3,200 pound payload. On November, 28th, 1936 the Fort William Times-Journal announced that manufacturing rights had been granted to Canadian Car and that the Fort William plant was , "a probable centre of operations". But other projects, including those brought about by the Second World War intervened and the aircraft was never built. However, as the war progressed favourably, arrangements were made in 1943 to build a newer Burnelli designed aircraft, the CBY-3. A new company, a wholly owned subsidiary of Canadian Car and Foundry was created in Montreal to build and market the aircraft. It was called Cancargo Aircraft Manufacturing Limited and Victor Drury was its President. Murray Semple was its Executive Vice President.

Canadian Car was encouraged in the project by a South American airline which initially wanted 20 CBY-3's built to their specifications and started to build the prototype in the Montreal factory in December, 1943. At some point during its construction the airline backed out of the deal, but work continued as best it could considering wartime priorities. By July, 1945, with the war in Europe over, the CBY-3, Registration CF-BEL-X (the X indicating experimental) was ready.

It was a twin engine (1200 hp), high wing monoplane with a classic Burnelli wide airfoil fuselage which made enough room for a cargo compartment forward and, towards the rear, 24 passengers seated in four rows. Cargo doors and separate passenger doors on each side gave access to the two payload areas. The cockpit was above and ahead of the cargo compartment, between the engines which thrust out ahead of it. There was a boom along each side which ran back to support the tail.

The war in Europe had ended in May, production was almost at an end in Fort William and the Burnelli was finally reaching the stage when a pilot was needed. The company moved Shorty to Montreal to work on this new venture and early that summer, the family had packed up and moved. There was still no highway across Northern Ontario and the move was complicated, unlike the earlier move to the west, by the addition of a family car. The answer lay on the water in the form of a passenger ship, the Noronic, which plied the Great Lakes, much in the manner of the ocean liners. A leisurely trip with excellent accommodation, good meals and the car tucked safely in the hold, saw the Hattons back in Montreal.

Pangborn, his bit for the cameras done, departed soon after that initial flight and thereafter testing was carried out by Shorty, who recorded air time in BEL-X almost daily throughout the remainder of July, all of August and the first half of October. There were problems and full certification was elusive for a number of reasons. It never left the ground from 17 October 1945 to January 9th, 1946. After nine days of flying in January, it went back into the hangar, where it stayed, being fitted with new more powerful (1450 hp Pratt & Whitney) engines, until May 10th. On that day Shorty recorded a brief ten minutes in the air, but two days later he flew it for close to an hour and then almost daily for the remainder of May, June and part of July.

There were a number of breaks. On Friday, April 5th, 1946, while the engineers were still working on BEL-X, Shorty took a flight that must have been slightly nostalgic for him. For the first time after several years of flying fighters and twin engine transports he was back in a bush plane, albeit a more advanced one than the Fairchilds in which he spent so many hours in the 30s.

The Noorduyn Norseman had been designed by Bob Noorduyn in the mid thirties and the first prototype flew from the St Lawrence river at Pointe Aux Trembles on 12 November, 1935. Over the years a number of variations had been produced by different companies. During the war years over

Clyde Edward Pangborn

Clyde "Upside Down" Pangborn was born in Washington State, USA on 28 October, 1894.

In 1917 he won his pilot's wings in the United States Army and following the First World War joined the Gates Flying Circus. He and his partner barnstormed around North America and Europe. He attracted attention by flying upside down and then establishing a world record for changing planes in mid-air. He participated in several long distance air races

His adventures with fellow pilot Roscoe Turner during the 1934 MacRobertson Air Race from London to Melbourne were depicted in the TV movie, "The Great Air Race" made in 1991.

He and a partner flew the first trans-Pacific Ocean flight, 4,500 miles non-stop in 41 hours and 13 minutes from Japan to Washington State in 1934.

In the late 1930s he was employed by the Bellanca Aircraft Corporation as a test pilot and by the Burnelli Corporation as a staff pilot.

During the Second World War he served as a civilian pilot in the Royal Air Force Ferry Command delivering aircraft across the Atlantic

800 of them had been sold to the United States Army Air Force and the RCAF which used them as utility aircraft. The military designation was C-64A and the most famous of them was the one in which big band leader Glenn Miller disappeared in 1944 on a flight from England to France. The military C-64A, in RCAF markings, can be seen at the National Aviation Museum in Ottawa.

In 1946 Canadian Car purchased the manufacturing rights and started turning them out at the St Laurent plant. This 1946 version was a civilianized model of the C-64A. It was called the Norseman V and, like its predecessors, was a typical bush plane - a high wing monoplane with a cabin which could carry cargo or, depending on the configuration, six or nine passengers. It was operated successfully on floats, wheels and skis.

Norseman V
Shorty tested 14 of these aircraft built at the Canadian Car and Foundry St. Laurent plant, 1946-48
Photo Courtesy Canada Aviation Museum

Over the next two years when he was not tied up with BEL-X, Shorty was to fly a number of them as they came off the production line. A typical test would consist of about 30 minutes flying from Cartierville. Sometimes, when the customer had ordered a float equipped version, he would then take the machine over to the Fairchild facility at Longuiel, where it would be fitted with floats whereupon he would check it out from the water. All told, he tested 14 Norseman Vs between April 1946 and July 1948.

On two occasions he was able to escape the Montreal area routine by ferrying a couple of them to Sault Ste Marie. On 24 June 1946 he made the six hour flight cruising along at about 140 miles per hour in CF-OBM to the Sault via Trout Mills, a seaplane base on the west end of Trout Lake at North Bay, Ontario. Then, on 11 and 12 July he repeated the performance with a sister aircraft, CF-OBL. Both had been purchased by the Ontario Department of Lands and Forests where they were used for a number of years by the "flying forest rangers" to patrol vast tracts of bush on the lookout for forest fires.

It is interesting to note that George F. "Buzz" Beurling a World War II

RCAF Ace was killed on 20 May 1948 when his Norseman V stalled while taking off from Rome en route to Israel where it was believed he was to join the Israeli Air Force. There has always been a mystery about the ownership and origin of the aircraft in which he died. Italian investigators identified the aircraft as N 69822, apparently a U.S. registration. However, U.S. records show that no such number was ever assigned to a Norseman. Either the Italians made a mistake in the number or, more likely, it had a false registration number to conceal its ownership in this slightly dubious venture.

The company, while concentrating on development of the CBY-3 and production of the Norseman was also engaged in some maintenance and repair of other aircraft and Shorty was called upon from time to time to check them out in the air.

In the summer of '45 he spent a couple of hours flying from Cartierville in an Avro Anson V, RCAF 11818. The Anson was a British designed twin engine trainer that had been built in large numbers by a variety of companies in Canada during the war. The twin 450 hp engines had an uneven sound which resulted in the unusual nickname given the machine by the airmen, "Limping Annie". The Mark V version was unusual in that the fuselage was made of moulded plywood, a technique that had been pioneered in Canada. Canadian Car and Foundry built 64 of them, including 11818 in 1944. There are at least two still in existence; one in the National Aviation Museum, Ottawa and the other in Canadian Warplane Heritage at Hamilton.

Avro Anson V
Similar to those built by Canadian Car and Foundry with a mouded plywood fudselage and flown by Shorty on different occasions in the summer of 1945.
RCAF Photo

Later that year he conducted similar flights in a PBY-5A registered in Iceland as TF-ICJ. This amphibious flying boat was known in Canada as the Canso and in the United States as the Catalina. Hundreds of them were built in Canada and elsewhere and they served in many countries. It was in a PBY-5A that Flight Lieutenant David Hornell, RCAF earned the Victoria Cross for his action in the sinking of a German submarine in June, 1944. Many of them continued in service in a variety of capacities for years after the war. In 1967, for example, a couple of them were being used as water bombers by the Newfoundland Forestry Service in Labrador. There is one in the National Aviation Museum, Ottawa.

PBY-5A
Canso / Catalina

These short adventures in flying other aircraft provided a change of pace, which is not to imply that life in Montreal was bad. Far from it. There were friends from the old days, Murray and Glad Semple, and the usual familiar crowd in the aviation business. The pay was good and the family was happily settled in a smart new home in an English speaking section of the city not far from the world famous shrine of Brother André. Daily he commuted the couple of miles to work at the Cartierville, and later Dorval, airports. It must have seemed strange, struggling with the Montreal rush hour traffic, but knowing that soon, when all those bankers, lawyers and clerks would be bent over paper in stuffy downtown offices, he would be high above it all, dodging the clouds.

The kids were growing and that provided Shorty with another concern, the worry of every father of an adolescent female. Joyce was showing signs of becoming a vivacious young lady and concern about the sort of people she was meeting and the young men who would soon appear on the scene had been a factor in their choice of residence. Suzanne was on the verge of adolescence and the baby, Ian, was at the age where he was just beginning to enjoy doing "men things" with his Dad. Montreal in those days was, as the Separatists told us so many years later, an excellent city "for the English". In the summer there were swimming picnics at Ile Bizard or visits to the Semple's summer place on Lake of two Mountains. With places like Mother Martin's and Ruby Foo's close at hand there was plenty of opportunity to have a night on the town. And, because so much of the testing on BEL consisted of short local flights, there was the luxury of going home to the family every night. A far cry from the prewar days when every flight was a venture into the unknown bush.

The only problems, it seemed, were with BEL-X, which had difficulty living up to expectations and, more important, government standards. Finally after months of fiddling and flying, she was granted a limited Domestic Certificate of Airworthiness and on March 1st, 1947, Shorty flew her for the first time without the experimental "X" after her name. From then on it was simply, CF-BEL and, while testing continued, the company began to move it around with a view to marketing. As part of the marketing strategy it was decided that it needed a more descriptive name than the rather technical sounding CBY3. After some consideration Vincent Burnelli and Murray Semple came up with "Loadmaster". Unfortunately the choice was open to jokes and Shorty privately referred to it as "The Toastmaster".

In the early spring of 1947 a chance to show it off and do some practical work presented itself. Attempts were being made to develop the potentially lucrative iron ore deposits in the Knob Lake area on the Labrador-Quebec border. The project had reached the stage where heavy equipment was needed but, with no roads or railroads the only way in was by air. Two old friends from the Canadian Airways days were working on the project and they were determined to show the value of heavy airlift under such circumstances. Bill Irvine was now an official in the Department of Civil Aviation and Babe Woollett was Canadian Pacific Airlines Superintendent of Operations in the Lower St Lawrence Region. Realizing at once that the use of float planes or even flying boats would be inadequate, their first priority was the establishment of an airport capable of handling large aircraft and they settled on what became the town of Shefferville. They also had to find aircraft to carry out the lift. The United States Air Force was anxious to try out some plywood skis they had developed for the DC3 Dakota and loaned three sets to CP to be fitted on their aircraft. The Bristol people in England were anxious to show off their newly built Bristol Freighter, which was designed for the nose to open completely thus permitting small vehicles to drive right into the cargo bay. And Cancargo was delighted to make the Loadmaster available. Canadian Pacific agreed to supply the fuel while Cancargo and Bristol provided the aircraft complete with crews. On March 13th, 1947 Shorty took BEL on a familiar route along the North Shore to Mont Joli, baie Comeau and Sept Isles where he had flown the mail so many years before.

At the Knob Lake site a winter airport was slowly taking shape. A small tractor, in bits and pieces, had been flown in by ski equipped Dakota and assembled. Once there it was used to develop a runway covered in impacted snow on the lake ice but capable of handling the wheeled Loadmaster and Bristol Freighter. The operation was mounted from Mont Joli where it was possible to renew an old friendship, recall the days gone by and, as Babe Woollett put it, "Sit around at night and booze in the hotel and shoot a line as pilots do". It was not long before Woollett made his joke about the name by pretending to confuse the Loadmaster with a popular kitchen utensil. Each time it came up Shorty who, as we have seen, already had his pet name for the machine, dutifully played the straight man by archly correcting him, "Loadmaster, old boy - Loadmaster - not Mixmaster".

The operation ended in early April when the impacted snow began to thaw and could no longer support the heavy aircraft. During it the Dakota skis broke and

CF-BEL in Labrador
The Burnelli CBY-3 Loadmaster carried over 28 tons of cargo to Knob Lake, Labrador in March and April, 1947

Hatton Family Photo

were returned to the USAF in splinters, the Bristol Freighter lost a wheel brace that had to be replaced and the Loadmaster, while remaining serviceable, proved to have limitations on its capabilities. Still, between mid March and April 8th, she had carried over 28 tons of cargo, mostly mining equipment, into this remote but rapidly developing area. All told the airlift, averaging 3,000 kilometres per day had moved 400 tons of equipment, including five tractors, two trucks, a snowblower, a road scraper and a jeep a distance of 560 kilometres.

Throughout the remainder of the spring of '47 and much of the summer there were a multitude of flights in the Montreal area and then on the 27th of August a flight to Uplands airport at Ottawa. On the 28th Shorty flew two separate demonstration flights, one for the Department of Transport, the other for the RCAF. Then it was back to Cartierville on the 29th for some photography.

Throughout the fall there was more flying in the Montreal area, including, in early September, a couple of demonstration flights for the Argentine Navy which came to nought.

Many of the test flights in the fall and early winter of 1947-48 were done with an engineer, Richard Richmond and various instruments on board. On 8 October Shorty's log records "feathered glides" and 'single engine climbs' on the

10th. During the feathered glide tests he would climb to 10,000 feet, feather the propellors and glide down at different speeds to lower altitudes while Richmond gathered the data needed to calculate the lift versus drag and thus the efficiency of the aircraft. Once, on the conclusion of such a flight, the propellors refused to unfeather and Shorty made ready to attempt a glide landing on frozen Lake of Two Mountains. He had no idea of the ice thickness and , fortunately, did not have to find out. After several attempts one propellor unfeathered and he was able to limp back to the airport on one engine.

While preparing to land at the conclusion of another flight with Richmond on board, one of the undercarriages did not come down. Shorty directed Richmond to open an access panel behind the pilot's seat and told him to find a cable with a ring attached. Once he found it, Richmond pulled the ring and the undercarriage fell down and locked into place. It was a designed feature and, fortunately, Shorty having done his homework, knew about it.

In late May 1948 he flew BEL to Washington DC via Burlington, Vermont and Teterboro, NewJersey. From the 24th to the 29th there were numerous demonstration flights in the Washington area and out over the Virginia countryside. A brief visit home and then off again to the USA, this time to Wright Field at Dayton, Ohio via Detroit. From the 16th to the 20th of June the United States Air Force at Wright- Patterson Air Force Base thoroughly evaluated the Loadmaster and concluded it was not for them. They were critical of several features including the lack of heat in the cabin where passengers might be carried and concluded that it could only have limited utility as a cargo plane.

By the 24th Shorty and BEL were back in Montreal. He spent the rest of the month testing a couple of Norseman V's.

There was more local flying in the Loadmaster in late August and early September and then from the 28th to the 30th of September a return trip to Sept Isles with stops at Mont Joli. Before 1948 ended Shorty took BEL to the RCAF Station at Rockcliffe. There, on 20th and 21st of December, he conducted a couple of short local flights and then returned to the Montreal area, not to Cartierville but to Dorval. The company, still hoping for a large sale, had acquired space there to manufacture more Loadmasters and from then on the Loadmaster operated from Dorval airport.

In January 1949, there were more local flights out of Dorval, including more single engine climb testing followed by no activity in February. On 5 March 1949 Shorty's log book records a one and a half hour flight out of Dorval with "G. Halderman and other CAR. Inspection, evaluation flight." There were further tests later that month and then in April, the last long trip for Shorty and BEL.

On April 2nd he flew her to the Lakehead and the following day to Brandon, Manitoba and the Canadian Joint Air Training Centre at nearby Rivers. CJATC was the military establishment, operated by the RCAF, at which the three services conducted joint training such as air support of ground forces, army aviation and airborne operations. It was the parachute school for the Canadian Army's airborne forces and, over the following week, Shorty piloted BEL around the area while parachutists jumped from her. He was particularly impressed with two of the jumpers, Major Sid Mooney of the Royal Canadian Artillery and Major Guy d'Artois, of the Royal 22nd Regiment. Both were experienced officers and during the war, D'Artois had parachuted into France to serve with the Underground where he had met the woman who was to become his wife. She too had jumped into Occupied France and served in the hidden fight against the Nazis. Shorty could not get over the fact that these two adventurers had settled down to a life of domestic bliss in the Married Quarters of a dull peacetime regular army. At that time neither of them could guess that, within a couple of years, D'Artois would be adding to his adventures as an infantry company commander in the hills of Korea.

After the Rivers adventure, Shorty and the Loadmaster spent two days in Winnipeg and then made the six hour flight direct to Dorval.

There was a bit more flying that year but not much. BEL never did get a Canadian Certificate of Airworthiness. In 1951 it went to the Burnelli Company in New York, received a new (US) registration and had a number of adventures before finally ending up in the Bradley Air Museum at Hartford Connecticut. It never started a dynasty. There were no more Loadmasters, only the one in which Shorty spent the last five years of his active flying life.

On July 31st, 1950, three months after his 51st birthday, he passed his semi-annual medical examination with flying colours but six months later when his licence was up for renewal, he let it lapse. Perhaps he, better than anyone else, recognized the growing limitations being placed on him by the years. Maybe he had admitted, at least to himself, that he was getting a little long in the tooth for a profession which had always been seen as a young man's business. He could not help smiling as he recalled that the two air forces in which he served had, as a matter of policy, concluded that thirty was a good upper age for pilots. He had reached that and twenty more and now he was faced with the prospect of staying on the ground. But he had many years yet in which to contribute to Canadian aviation.

Cold War

The word from Cookie was disturbing and food for thought. It certainly was worth a phone call to Tom Cowley, now retired from the RCAF and working in Ottawa as the Department of Transport's Director of Air Services, to find out if he knew anything. He confirmed that he too had heard the rumour. While there was nothing official, Shorty's employer was, indeed, suspected by some people of having Communist connections. Nothing sufficient to warrant any official action but enough, nevertheless to, make him and, perhaps, those who worked for him, slightly suspect.

Shorty had first met the man in question during the war when he had journeyed to Fort William on a trip to sell components from his small technical company to Canadian Car. He was a pleasant fellow and in time made it clear to Shorty that, should he ever leave Canadian Car, there might be work for him at his company. When the Loadmaster project had fizzled out, Shorty had joined him in his Toronto plant and the family had left Montreal to take up residence in a newly built house on the farm at Winona.

Life in Winona was pleasant enough. True, it was a bit of a distance from the office, but the drive along the as yet uncongested Queen Elizabeth Highway was not bad and, besides the family, there were old friends in the area. Dave Boyd's wife, Mary, had died, but he had remarried and was living in nearby St Catherines, just down the highway. At the end of the war he had joined the John Inglis company and was doing for washing machine production that which he had done so well on the manufacture of Hawker Hurricanes and Avro Lancasters. Cookie, who had recently married Fran Walker, an attractive widow with a young son, was working out of Toronto, as a sales representative. He was still with Canadian Car, which was now building busses at the Fort William plant.

In 1951, the greatest fear in the western World was Communism. While the average Canadian knew little of the details of the Communist Manifesto and only one in a thousand had the foggiest idea of what Karl Marx had actually said in his later dreary tome, "Capital", everyone knew that his ideas, embodied in the Union of Soviet Socialist Republics, which most thought of as Russia, were bad. Stalin was in charge of things in that part of the world and, although he had been hailed, along with Churchill and Roosevelt, as one of The Big Three Allied leaders during World War II, his actions since then had given the world enough evidence to conclude that his intentions were not in the best interests of democratic government. It was commonly believed that he controlled a tightly disciplined international organization the aim of which was to impose Soviet control on the world. There was evidence to support the idea, starting with the iron grip under which the Soviet Union held those parts of Europe and Asia it had "liberated" during the war.

Canada had been rudely introduced to this new world order in 1946 when a Soviet file clerk, Igor Gouzenko, had defected from the Soviet Embassy in Ottawa along with over a hundred documents which proved, beyond any doubt, that Allied secrets had been going illegally to Moscow for many years. A subsequent Royal Commission and investigation by the Royal Canadian Mounted Police revealed that an extensive spy ring was operating in Canada. It included citizens from every walk of life: a respected industrialist - a Member of Parliament - scientists - military people - members of the civil service including a mousy little widow who worked as a clerk in a government office. It also clearly indicated that there were others who could not be identified, at least not to the extent that they could be prosecuted. There was some understanding of those who had taken part in the espionage. The Soviets had been our Allies during the war and, for a certain kind of idealist, there was an appeal in the theory of Communism which, completely ignoring human nature, assumed that all humans wanted to be equal. While Canadians avoided the hysteria that developed in the United States with Senator Joseph McCarthy's witch hunts for "Un American Activity", official Canada quietly kept an eye on them.

In the summer of 1950 there was further evidence that International Communism was intent on conquering the world. The tiny Asian nation of Korea had been divided at the end of the war into two sections. The one in the south was occupied by the Americans and had adopted a U.S. style of government. In the North, which had been occupied by the Soviet Union, a Communist leader, Kim Il Sungh, had been installed by the Soviets and, in June of 1950, his forces invaded the South. The United Nations, under U.S. leadership, had responded with troops and by that winter, when Shorty was working for this new Toronto-based small manufacturing firm, young Canadians were dying in the rice paddies of Korea. Their enemies were the soldiers of North Korea and China but no one thought of them in that way. Everyone knew that they were Communists.

The suggestion that he might be working for an enemy was alarming. Aside from the limited opportunities that a technically oriented company might have in that atmosphere, there was something personally unpalatable about being involved with it and Shorty decided that he would rather be employed elsewhere. The problem was where .

To make matters worse he came down with a familiar illness, pneumonia. It could not have come at a worse time. With no company health plan to help out and, in those days before universal health care, no other financial support to pay for expensive drugs, it presented a major problem. Once again family support materialized in the form of a five hundred dollar cheque from Dougie which saw them through. Then, when he recovered from this latest bout, a suggestion from Dave Boyd paid off.

From the point of view of a man skilled in the production of aircraft, the Cold War had its blessings. The nation was rearming and a company that was expanding to produce aircraft for the rapidly growing RCAF had emerged in Toronto. A.V.Roe Canada had taken over the wartime facilities of Victory Aircraft, where the Lancasters had been built. By 1951 it was working on two major products: the development of a new airliner equipped with jet engines and a fighter for the Air Force. Included on the staff were a number of acquaintances from the tightly knit aviation community who were well aware of his outstanding work as Chief Inspector at Canadian Car both in Fort William and at Montreal and Shorty was able to get an aviation job, on the ground. In 1951 he was hired by A.V.Roe Canada to be the company's Chief Experimental and Test Flight Inspector.

The new fighter was the CF100, an all weather twin jet engine machine which had been designed to specifications established by the RCAF and when Shorty joined the company it was having a lot of teething problems. The prototype had been first flown in January 1950 by test pilot Bill Waterton but the wheels would not retract. Later there were problems with the wings buckling. After much testing and redesigning to say nothing of internal problems at Avro, Waterton had been fired. Then in April 1951, the prototype crashed near London, Ontario during high speed tests. The pilot, Flight Lieutenant Bruce Warren of the RCAF and a company observer, Robert Ostrander were both killed.

CF-100 Mark 4

Photo Courtesy Canada Aviation Museum

By June of 1951 the Mark 2 version of the machine, equipped with new Orenda engines which had also been developed by Avro Canada, made its maiden flight and in October several Mk 2's were delivered to the RCAF where they were to be known formally as CF-100 Canucks. In November, after working on them for a while, the airmen informally renamed the machine CF-Clunk and they were returned to Avro for further work.

The further work was so extensive that it warranted a change in designation and finally, in the summer of 1952, the Mark 3 CF-100 was delivered to the air force. It suffered from problems with the fuel feed and could not shake its unflattering name to which were now added two others, "CF-Zilch" and "The Lead Sled". While there were technical problems with the aircraft not all of the blame for its reputation could be laid on Avro. In later years RCAF officers admitted that the pilots really were not up to flying a high performance all weather machine. Nor did they understand the complexities of aircraft development and, some of them at least, expected a perfect aeroplane. No such machine has ever existed.

All of which was disturbing for the people at the Avro plant who believed they were producing a good fighter. Shorty, who had personal experience on the first Canadian designed fighter, the Gregor, in the late 30s, was most enthusiastic about this new jet. In time a number of problems were corrected and the CF-100 Mk 3 went into squadron service on April 1st 1953. By June of that year the Mark 4 version was being produced at the rate of one per day and Shorty was kept busy inspecting them before signing off to the two production test pilots; Chris Pike and Stan Haswell.

There was also a change in the family during 1953. Joyce, now a grown woman, had fallen in love with a young naval officer, Sub Lieutenant Robin Allen, and on October 31st they were married in St. Andrew's Church, Grimsby. It was a formal wedding in the best traditions of the Royal Canadian Navy with Groom, Best Man and ushers in uniform, complete with swords. Shorty was quietly pleased to find that he was able to dress in his old Morning Suit, the one in which he had been married, just a few miles away at Winona, twenty-three years before. A year later he and Gwen reached another significant milestone in their lives when they became grandparents on the birth of Tony Allen.

At the plant, Avro was looking to the future and development work had started on two new projects in which he would soon become involved. The designers were working on plans for a new fighter to be known as the CF-105. And there was a completely new idea which would, in time, be called the Avrocar. It was a ground cushion vehicle which, when finally developed would look like a flying

Avrocar
Photo Court'sy Canada Aviation Museum

saucer with its completely circular fuselage.

By this time the daily commute from Winona to Malton was getting tougher and they found a new place to live that was a bit closer, on Lakeshore Boulevard in Burlington. A year later, having received a small inheritance from Gwen's mother, they bought the first home they had ever owned on Wilson Avenue in Burlington.

In January, 1955, production had slowed down and there were layoffs at the plant which resulted in some labour problems but the following month it became necessary to replace the canopies on the CF-100 fleet and the company was trying hard to sell it overseas. Late in the year two of the company's top test pilots, Jan Zurakowski and Glen Lynes demonstrated the Mark 4 version at the prestigious annual Farnborough Air Show in England. The demonstrations were successful in that, in due time, Belgium purchased 53 machines. A month later Lynes was killed when the Mark 5 machine he was testing crashed.

In the meantime work was progressing on the new CF-105, the details of which were very secret. In his capacity as Chief Experimental Inspector, Shorty was privy to some of the secrets and was astonished one day when Gwen showed him a drawing done by eleven year old Ian who, like most young boys, was fascinated with aeroplanes. It was a reasonably accurate representation of the top secret CF-105. Needless to say, the youngster had not penetrated the secu-

CF-105
Avro Arrow
Photo Courtesy Canada Aviation Museum

rity system at Avro. His drawing was merely the product of an active imagination.

Finally in October 1957, the new CF-105, christened The Arrow, was revealed to the public and flew for the first time on March 28th, 1958 with Zurakowski at the controls. There were other tests that year and several more were built. But it all came to an end on Friday, February 20th, 1959 when the government cancelled the contract. Avro immediately fired everybody; 14,528 people, many of them the most skilled aircraft workers in the world.

Shorty may well have reflected on the fact that only three fighter planes had ever been developed in Canada and he was, perhaps, the only person to have worked intimately on all three. The CF-100 saw a number of years of peacetime service, but the Gregor and the Arrow were never produced. It may have given him cause for thought on the future in Canada of the industry in which he had spent most of his life. It is certain that his feelings matched those of everyone else at Avro. There has been much controversy over the decision to cancel the development of this new aircraft which, by everyone's admission, was years ahead of its time. Any number of books have been written and arguments advanced, both for and against. Trying to understand the event is further clouded by people with a political bent, trying to achieve other, unstated, aims. Whatever the higher reasons for the decisions made in government, and in the company, the practical result for far too many people was the loss of their livelihood.

Once again, Shorty was out of work. There is nothing so devastating as losing a job and it is doubly so when you are sixty years old. It really is too late to start over again and most employers believe, rightly or wrongly, that anyone that age is incapable of learning new skills and ways. In later years the government would introduce a national pension plan and enlightened companies would introduce special arrangements for employees who are no longer needed. None of these existed in 1959 and Shorty, with a family to support, had to find a job. For a while he tried selling mutual funds and then he was able to obtain work with de Havilland, the other aircraft manufacturing company in the Toronto area. De Havilland was doing well with its new line of Short Take off and Landing (STOL) aircraft and hired a number of former Avro employees.

In 1960, a tragic event in Halifax devastated the whole family. Joyce's husband, Robin, died unexpectedly, leaving her with three small children. She came to live with Shorty and Gwen in Burlington but the house proved to be a bit small for a family of six, three of them under the age of ten and in 1962, Joyce bought a larger home on Partridge Avenue in nearby Aldershot.

As the years passed, the other children married and there were more grandchildren, all in the area, to the delight of the grandparents.

On the social side Shorty was rapidly becoming a member of the unofficial fraternity of aviation "Old Boys". In 1961, George Wakeman organized a number of aviation pioneers to make a presentation to Mrs. J.A.McCurdy, the widow of the aviation pioneer who had made the first controlled flight by a British subject in the British Empire when he flew the Silver Dart at Baddeck NS on 23 February 1909. They gave her a framed portrait, bearing the following inscription:

> *"We remember with admiration John McCurdy our friend and colleague who by his historic flight in the aeroplane 'Silver Dart' and his subsequent pioneering flights showed us and men of many nations the art of flight using a heavier than air machine"*

It was signed by, in Wakeman's words, "a fair cross-section of service and civilian pilots, heads of the aviation industry and education in Canada":

Geo Wakeman	*C.M.McEwen*
V.J.Hatton	*Raymond Collishaw*
R.Dodds	*Robert A.Logan*
W.A.Seymour	*Basil W.Hobbs*
G.R.McGregor	*T.R.Loudon*
Jack Sanderson	*Sandy MacDonald*
P.C.Garrat	*O.C.S Wallace*
W.A.Curtis	*R.H.Bibby*
C.H.Dickens	*Alan G.Wingate*
Harry McLean	

In 1964 Shorty celebrated his 65th birthday and formally became a senior citizen but continued to work for another three years. In 1967 at the time of his retirement from de Havilland he spoke to the Canadian Aviation Historical Society on his flying adventures over the years. Ian had driven him over to Toronto for this event and stayed to hear the talk. For the first time in his life he discovered some of the details of his father's working life. While he knew his Dad had been a pilot he had no idea of the scope of his career, until he heard the speech, listened to the questions posed by these aviation enthusiasts and heard his father's knowledgeable answers.

As the years passed the old friends faded away. He and Gwen moved into a small home on Claredge Drive in Burlington and he coped with increasing age with typical logic, common sense and self discipline.

When his car rolled down a drive because he had failed to set the parking brake, he concluded that he was becoming dangerous behind the wheel and gave up driving, just as abruptly as he had given up flying.

When he sensed that his consumption of alcohol should be controlled, he established a rule of never having a drink before five in the afternoon. And when the life long susceptibility to pneumonia manifested itself in Emphysema, he stopped smoking. This must have been the hardest of all. He had smoked incessantly since those days so long ago in the trenches when Wild Woodbines were ten for a penny, taking the cigarette from the package, turning it in his hand, tapping it on the face of his wrist watch and putting it, with great satisfaction, into his mouth.

On June 21st, 1980 he and Gwen celebrated their Golden Wedding Anniversary with a grand party at Sue's home in Burlington. All the family gathered and the children had managed to find an old friend from the Canadian Airways days. Emile Patrault, retired in Ottawa, sent a bottle of good Scotch for the celebration, but there were no others from the old days. A few years before there had been a memorable long weekend in the Laurentians with Cookie, Jim Davis, Dave Boyd and their families but now they were all gone.

As the years passed the poison gas in the trenches, the cigarettes and the pneumonia took their toll and his lungs grew worse. In time, he had to keep an oxygen tank close by. He was hospitalized several times and then, in the spring of 1991, at the time of his 92nd birthday he was admitted to the Joseph Brant Memorial Hospital in Burlington where he was placed on a life support system. On the 27th of April he spoke with the family and urged Ian to look after his mother who was, in his words, "very strong, but she still needs to be looked after".

Then, as he had stopped flying when he sensed that he could no longer do it properly, he stopped living.

Appendix A

THE SILVER CIGARETTE BOX
Presented to
V.J.Hatton
by the
Pilots of Canadian Airways
on the occasion of his marriage
June 21st 1930

R.H.Bibby
Richard Henry Bibby
First Canadian commercial pilot's licence issued 20 May, 1928 (# 277)
Worked for:
Ontario Provincial Air Service
Sky View Air Lines Ltd, Chippewa ON
Canadian Airways Ltd
A.B. Purvis, Montreal
Canadian Vickers Ltd Montreal
Canadair Ltd, Montreal
Died 20 March, 1961 at Montreal PQ

E.C.Burton
Edward Cherry Burton
First Canadian commercial pilot's licence issued 29 June, 1924 (# 198)
Worked for:
Ontario Provincial Air Service
Toronto Flying Club
National Air Transport Ltd, Toronto
Old Canadian Airways Ltd
Canadian Airways Ltd
London Flying Club
Ottawa Flying Club
Dominion Skyways Ltd, Montreal
Amos Air Service, Amos PQ
Leavens Bros, Air Service Ltd, Toronto ON

G.C. Drury
G. Chipman Drury
Worked for
Canadian Vickers
Canadian Airways Ltd
Canadian Car and Foundry

Ronald F. George
Ronald Frederick George
First Canadian commercial pilot's licence 10 January, 1929 (#415)
Worked for :
International Airways of Canada Ltd, Hamilton ON
Canadian Airways Ltd
Trans Canada Airlines

A.F. Ingram
Arthur Ferguson "Peggy" Ingram
First Canadian commercial pilot's licence 23 October, 1928 (# 371)
Worked for:
International Airways of Canada Ltd, Hamilton ON
Canadian Airways Ltd

W. Irvine
William Herbert Irvine
First Canadian commercial pilot's licence 20 May, 1928 (# 290)
Worked for:
Ontario Provincial Air Service
Canadian Transcontinental Airways, Ltd, Montreal
Canadian Airways Ltd

Dominion Skyways Ltd Montreal
Laurentian Air Services Ltd, Ottawa
Department of Transport

B. Martin
Bernard Martin
First Canadian commercial pilot's licence 22 May, 1929 (# 479)
Worked for:
Curtiss-Reid Aircraft Ltd, Montreal
Canadian Airways, Ltd
Fairchild Aircraft Ltd, Longueil PQ
Died in crash at Longueil PQ 17 June 1933

Red H. Mulock
Colonel Redford Henry "Red" Mulock, CBE, DSO, ADC
First Canadian to qualify for a pilot's licence (#1103) in British Military
Worked for:
Canadian Vickers
Canadian Airways Ltd
Canadian Car and Foundry

J.R.Robertson
John Roderick Robertson
First Canadian commercial pilot's licence 3 May, 1921 (# 115)
Worked for:
Canadian Airways Ltd

A. Schneider
Alexander S. Schneider
First Canadian commercial pilot's licence 21 July, 1928 (# 327)
Canadian Transcontinental Airways Ltd, Quebec PQ
Canadian Airways Ltd
Self employed
Fairchild Aircraft Ltd Longueil PQ

H.C.W.Smith
Harold Clifford Wesley "Deacon" Smith
First Canadian commercial pilot's licence 11 October, 1920 (# 57)
Worked for:
International Aerial Transport Ltd Toronto ON
Jack V. Elliot, Hamilton, ON
Ontario Provincial Air Service
Gillies Air Service Ltd, Kitchener ON
Interprovincial Airways Ltd, Montreal PQ

Canadian Airways Ltd
Canadian Colonial Airways Ltd, Montreal PQ
A.E.Wicks, Cochrane ON
Killed in crash on 10 August, 1941 in Scotland

R.Vachon
Joseph Pierre Romeo Vachon
First Canadian commercial pilot's licence 7 March, 1923 (# 182)
Worked for:
Laurentide Air Services Ltd, Montreal PQ
Ontario Provincial Air Service
Canadian Transcontinental Airways Ltd, Quebec PQ
Canadian Airways Ltd
Quebec Airways Ltd, Montreal PQ
Trans Canada Airlines
Air Transport Board, Ottawa
Died at Quebec, PQ on 18 December, 1954

O.S.Wallace Jr
Oates Crosby Saunders Wallace
First Canadian commercial pilot's licence 4 February 1921 (# 99)
Worked for:
Canadian Airways Ltd

Appendix B

SHORTY'S AIRCRAFT IN MUSEUMS

The National Aviation Museum
Ottawa (Rockcliffe) ON

G-CAUA
DeHAVILLAND DH 60X MOTH
Saturday, 2 November, 1929 Toronto-Hamilton

G-CART
FAIRCHILD FC-2W-2
24 Mar 1930 mail Toronto-Montreal

RCAF 5584
HAWKER HURRICANE XII
Tested at Fort William Nov 42

CF-ATF
JUNKERS W34
12 Aug 38 Senneterre - Toronto via Orillia where he lost the ladder in Lake Couchiching.

CF-TCA
LOCKHEED 10A ELECTRA
Fall 1937 Winnipeg TCA Training Course (original registration CF-TCC)

CF-AMB
STEARMAN 4EM
(This is NOT the orginal AMB)
First flew the original on Wed 11 Jun 1930 Montreal
The aircraft in which Gwen flew as an unauthorized passenger on New Year's Eve, 1931

OTHER TYPES HE FLEW WHICH ARE IN THE NATIONAL AVIATION MUSEUM

AVRO 504K
Was seriously injured in the crash of a 504K on 9 Oct, 1922
Over the years in the RAF and RCAF he compiled about 300 hours in this type and AVRO 504N

AVRO AVIAN
10 hours in this type listed in log

AVRO ANSON V
2 hours in this type, 11818 (RCAF?), at Canadian Car Montreal in Aug 45

DeHAVILLAND DH 80A PUSS MOTH
Flew type CF-AGV owned by Cdn Airways between 1932-35 in Quebec

NOORDYUN NORSEMAN V
Tested fifteen Montreal 1946-48

STINSON SR RELIANT
Flew type CF-BGO and CF-BGP 2-10 Sep 38

Western Canada Aviation Museum
Winnipeg, Manitoba

CF-AKT
FAIRCHILD 71 (Converted from FC-2W-2)
Forced landing at Seboies, Maine enroute St John - St Hubert with Gwen as passenger 28 July, 1930 and flown on many other flights in the early 30s.

Reynolds-Alberta Museum
Wetaskiwan, AB

NC 18388 (Later CF-BVE)
BARKLEY GROW T8P-1
National demonstration tour October, 1938

Bradley Air Museum
Hartford, Connecticut

CF-BEL (later U.S.registration)
BURNELLI CBY-3 LOADMASTER
Tested 19 Jul 45 through 1949

Shuttleworth Aircraft Collection
Bedfordshire, England

Z7015
HAWKER HURRICANE Mk I
Tested at Fort William, 18 January, 1941
Rebuilt and test flown on 16 September, 1996

U.S. Naval Aviation Museum
Pensacola, Florida

GRUMMAN G-23 (GOBLIN)
Built by Canadian Car & Foundry, Fort William, ON, 1938
Type tested in 1939 and 1940 at Fort William, ON

Appendix C

SHORTY
NOTES ON SOURCES

1   Two principle sources of the material in this book are Shorty's pilot log books. Only two have survived the years. One covers the period from June 1929 when he first joined International Airways to September 1931. The second contains details of his instrument flying in 1933 and in 1936 as well as all flying from May 1938 to his last flights in 1949.

2   I had extensive interviews, a few on the phone, with, and countless notes from, his widow Gwen from 1993 to 2004.

3   Personal audio and videotapes of Shorty and his brother Bill Hatton reminiscing which are held by the Hatton Family

4   Royal Air Force record of military service: F/O V.J. Hatton

5   Air Ministry (Great Britain) Pilot's Licence and Certificate of Competency # 1307

6   Ministry of Defence (Great Britain) Air Historical Branch letter dated 23 Sep, 1993

7   Ministry of Defence (Great Britain) letter HB(A)/6/2 dated 8 Oct, 1993

8   National Army Museum, Chelsea, London letter dated 29 Nov, 1993

9   The History of the London Rifle Brigade, 1859 - 1919
London: Constable & Co. Ltd.
1921

10   The Special Air Service
Philip Warner
William Kimber : London
1971

11   They Called it Passchendaele
Lyn MacDonald
Penguin Books

12   Voices and Images of The Great war
Lyn MacDonald
1991 Penguin Books

13   Marshall Foch, A Sudy in Leadership
Lt Col T.M. Hunter
Queen's Printer and Controller of Stationery
Ottawa, 1961

14   Armed Forces in Peacetime
Robin Higman
G.T. Foulis & Co., Ltd.
London, 1962

15   Aircraft of the Royal Air Force Since 1918
Owen Thetford
Putnam and Company, London
7th Edition, 1979

16 Pictorial History of the RAF, Volume One 1918-1939
John W.R. Taylor
Aeco Publishing Company Inc.
New York 1968

17 The Creation of A National Air Force
The Official Hisdtory of The Royal Canadian Air Force, Volume II
W.A.B.Douglas
University of Toronto Press in cooperation with the Department of National Defence and the Government Publishing Centre, Supply and Services
Ottawa, 1986

18 The Canadians At War 1939/45
The Reader's Digest Association (Canada) Ltd.
1969

19 Canadian Civil Aircraft Register 1920-29
John R. Ellis
Canadian Aviation Historical Society

20 Canadian Civil Aircraft Register 1929-45
John R. Ellis
Canadian Aviation Historical Society

21 The First 500 Canadian Civil Pilots
K.M.Molson
Canadian Aviation Historical Society

22 Pioneering In Canadian Air Transport
K.M. Molson
1974

23 Canada's Flying Heritage
Frank H. Ellis
University of Toronto Press, 1954

24 The De Havilland Story
Fred W.Hotson
Canav Books
Toronto, 1983

25 Audio tape
Walter "Babe" Woollett
Jun 1993

26 Walter "Babe" Woollett
Telephone Interview
Jun 1993

27 Have A Banana
Walter "Babe" Woollett
Turner-Warwick Publications, 1989

Appendix C
Notes on Sources

28	Canadian Aircraft Since 1909 K.M. Molson & H.A. Taylor Canada's Wings Stittsville, ON, 1979
29	K.E. Molson Interviews Aug, 1993
30	Hamilton Spectator 7 June, 1929 14 December, 1931 21 December, 1932 13 February, 1963
31	Winnipeg Free Press 22 January, 1932
32	Canadian Aviation Magazine February, 1932 July, 1932 March, 1940
33	And I Shall Fly The Flying Memoirs of Z. Lewis Leigh Canav Books Toronto, 1985
34	Canadian Civil Aviation Pilot's Licence # 16 1 April, 1936
35	Canada's National Aviation Museum Kenneth M. Molson National Aviation Museum National Museum of Science and Technology Ottawa, 1988
36	125 years of Canadian Aeronautics G.A. Fuller, J.A. Griffith, K.M. Molson Canadian Aviation Historical Society Willowdale, 1983
37	Walter Henry Letters re Barkley-Grow aircraft dated 3 December and 14 December, 1993
38	History of Canadian Airports T.M. McGrath Lugus Publications in cooperation with Transport Canada and the Canadian Government Publishing Centre, Supply and Services Canada, 1992
39	Fort William Times-Journal 28 November, 1936 16 April, 1938 30 May, 1938 2 June, 1936

            29 October, 1938
            3 November, 1938
            7 November, 1938
            2 January, 1940
            25 May, 1940
            24 October, 1940
            6 June, 1941
            14 February, 1947

40   Photo 242 Squadron, RAF
        January, 1940
        National Archives PA 123590

41   General Dynamics Aircraft and Their Predecessors
        John Wegg
        Naval Institute Press

42   Grumman Sixty years of Excellence
        Bill Gunston
        Orion Books, A Division of Crown Publishuing, Inc.
        New York, 1988

43   William J. Wheeler
        Letter to V.J. Hatton dated January, 1967

44   UTDC
        Canadian Car Thunder Bay Works

45   A History of Thunder Bay
        Joseph M.Mauro
        Privately Published

46   William P. Onchulenko
        Letter Burlington Spectator
        March, 1993

47   Historic Headlines
        P. Berton (Ed)
        McLelland & Stewart Ltd.
        Toronto, 1967

48   Shutting Down The National Dream
        A.V.Roe and The Tragedy of the Avro Arrow
        Greig Stewart
        McGraw-Hill Ryerson
        1988

49   R.W.Bradford
        Letter dated 12 Nov 1993

50   Alan Walker (H.Cook's step son)
        Telephone interview December, 1993

51   Ian M. Hatton
        Interviews September, 1993

Appendix C
Notes on Sources

52	Joyce (Hatton) Calverly and Collett Calverley
	Interviews November, 1993
53	Jill Warwick (R.Bibby's step daughter)
	Telephone interview December, 1993
54	Peggy (Graham/Drury) Scully
	Telephone interview January, 1994
55	Aeroplane Monthly
	February, 1994
54	Northern Flight
	Vol 2, Number 3,
	October 1994
55	Robert S. Grant (Aviation writer on Fairchild aircraft)
	Telephone interview, November, 1994
56	Aeroplane Monthly
	October, 1997
57	Voyageurs of the Air
	J.R.K.Main
	Department of Transport, Ottawa, 1967
58	Correspondence from Brian Johannesson, including an article from Canadian Aviation Magazine of May 1980 regarding the Laird CF-APY
59	Conversations and correspondence with Geoff Bennet, 2003
60	The Barrie Examiner, 8 November, 1928.
61	Barrie Northern Advance, 8 November, 1928.
62	E Mail from Pierre Vachon, son of Romeo Vachon in May, 2004
63	The Air mails of Canada and Newfoundland
	A Volume in the Sixth Edition of the American Air Mail Catalogue
	American Air Mail Society, 1997
64	I have viewed countless web sites devoted to pioneer aviation on the internet. Some come and go with alarming regularity and it would be a monumental, and pointless, task to list them all. Suffice it to say that almost anything mentioned in the book can be found somewhere on the internet.

Index

A

A.V.Roe Canada : 125
Adye, George F.G. : 92, 100
Air Ministry Acceptance Pilot : 99
Aircraft, Individual
    AE 962 : 105
    AG 325 : 105
    BW 835 : 105
    CF- ACT : 28
    CF- TCC : 78
    CF-AAA : 24
    CF-AAT : 68
    CF-AAX : 28
    CF-ACO : 28, 57, 70
    CF-ACY : 41, 45, 70, 82
    CF-AEO : 73
    CF-AET : 67
    CF-AHG : 84
    CF-AKT : 43, 136
    CF-ALM : 64-66
    CF-AMB : 35, 46, 47, 135
    CF-AMC : 35, 46, 47
    CF-APG : 84
    CF-APJ : 65-66, 83
    CF-APY : 74
    CF-AQY : 74
    CF-ASE : 54, 64-66
    CF-ASF : 54, 64-66
    CF-ATF : 84, 135
    CF-AVJ : 73
    CF-AWU : 84
    CF-AYE : 83
    CF-BAF : 78
    CF-BDF : 83
    CF-BEL : 113, 119, 122, 136
    CF-BEL-X : 114
    CF-BFL : 79, 82
    CF-BGO : 88, 93
    CF-BGP : 88, 93
    CF-BKP : 82
    CF-BLK : 89
    CF-BMB : 92, 102
    CF-BMV. See NC 18469
    CF-BVE. See NC 18388
    CF-OBG : 116
    CF-OBL : 116
    CF-OBM : 116
    CF-TCA : 79, 135
    CF-TCB : 78
    G-AAFW : 29
    G-AWLW. See RCAF 5545
    G-CANF : 43
    G-CARR : 39
    G-CART : 28, 135
    G-CATU : 23
    G-CAUA : 32, 135
    G-CAWB : 26
    G-CAWF : 28
    N2527 : 99
    NC 18388 : 86, 136
    NC 18469 : 93, 94
    P5170. See NC 18388
    P5208 : 102
    RCAF 11818 : 117
    RCAF 176 : 61-66
    RCAF 339 : 104
    RCAF 5447 : 111
    RCAF 5545 : 111
    RCAF 5584 : 111, 135
    RCAF 758. See NC 18469
    Z7015 : 111, 136
Aircraft, Types
    Avro 504K : 9-18, 135
    Avro 504N : 18
    Avro 549 Aldershot : 14, 15
    Avro 627 : 47
    Avro Anson V : 117
    Avro Avian : 135
    Avrocar : 126
    Barkley-Grow T8P-1 : 86
    Bristol Freighter : 119
    Burnelli CBY-3 : 113
    Burnelli UB-14 : 114
    C-64A. See Norseman V
    Canso : 117
    CF-100 Canuck : 125
    CF-105 Arrow : 126, 127
    Curtis-Reid Courier : 64-66

DC3 Dakota : 119
DH 60 Moth : 17, 135
DH 75 Hawk Moth : 29
DH 83C Fox Moth : 84
DH 84 Dragon : 65
DH 89 Dragon Rapide : 73
DH Cirrus Moth : 24
DH Gipsy Moth : 24
DH Puss Moth : 61, 136
Fairchild 51 : 27
Fairchild 71, 71B, 71C : 28
Fairchild FC-2 : 23, 27
Fairchild FC-2W-2 : 28, 135
FDB-1 Gregor : 92, 101, 128
FE 2B Bomber : 22
Fokker Super Universal : 26, 27
Goblin. See Grumman G-23
Grumman G-23 : 89, 103, 136
Hawker Hurricane : 105, 106, 135, 136
Junkers W-34 : 68, 135
Laird LC-200 : 74
Lancaster bombers : 106
Lockheed 10A Electra : 78, 135
Maple Leaf : 101
Noorduyn Norseman : 115
Norseman IV : 83
Norseman V : 116, 136
PBY-5A : 117
Pitcairn PA-6 Mailwing : 28
Pregnant Frog. See Grumman G-23
SBW Curtis Helldiver : 112
Sea Hurricane : 105
Siskin Fighters : 24
Stearman 4EM2 : 34, 37, 135
Stearman C-2 : 39
Stinson Reliant : 88, 136
Vickers Vimy : 14, 16
Waco Ten : 42
Aldergrove : 15
Allen, Robin : 126, 128
Allen, Tony : 126
Anticosti Island : 60, 80
Argentine Navy : 120
Aviation Corporation of Canada : 25

B

Baddeck NS : 129
Battle of Britain : 102, 103
Belanger, Romeo : 60
Bersimis : 59
Bibby, R.H. "Dick" : 24, 30, 33, 47, 60, 68, 70, 99, 111, 129, 131
Binnett, Dr. : 67
Bishop's Field : 97
Bone, Freddie : 75
Boyd, David : 90, 97, 102, 106, 123, 130
Bradford, R.W. : 9, 57, 113
Bradley Air Museum : 122
Brandon, Manitoba : 122
British Army
    28th London Regiment : 5
    5th Army : 3
    Non-Commissioned Officeers : 7
    Special Air Service : 5
    The Artist's Rifles : 5
    The London Rifle Brigade : 2, 8
    XVII Corps : 4
British Commonwealth Air Training Plan : 41, 85
Brownville : 39
Bulman, George : 97, 108
Burlington : 127, 130
Burnelli, Vincent : 113
Burton, E.C. "Ed" : 31, 51, 132

C

Cagney, Jimmy : 105
Cambrai : 107
Camp Borden : 19, 61
Canada Aviation Museum : 32
Canadian Air Express : 48
Canadian Airways. : 26, 59
Canadian Aviation Historical Society : 129
Canadian Aviation magazine, : 100
Canadian Car & Foundry : 114
Canadian Car and Foundry : 66, 87, 97, 102, 123
Canadian Joint Air Training Centre : 122
Canadian National Exhibition : 105
Canadian Pacific Airlines : 85

Canadian Transport Pilot's Licence : 72
Canadian Warplane Heritage : 117
Canadian Warplane Heritage Museum : 111
Capreol, Leigh : 99
Cartierville : 118
Caterpillar Club : 51
Chateau Frontenac : 70
Chez Maurice : 42
Chibougamau : 68
Chief Experimental and Test Flight Inspector : 125
cigarette : 6, 130
Collishaw, Raymond : 129
Communist : 124
Cook, Horace "Cookie" : 31, 44, 60, 64-66, 88, 109, 123, 130
Cowley, A.T. "Tom" : 61, 72, 111, 123
Cowman, Jean : 53, 54
Cramm, Sydney : 97
Curtis, W.A. : 129

D

d'Artois, Major Guy : 122
Davis, Jim : 60-66, 130
De Havilland : 128
Denman, Dougie : 70, 97. See Glassco, Douglas "Dougie"
Denman, R.O. "Bob" : 22, 24, 31, 55, 98
Detroit : 26, 89
Dickens, C.H "Punch" : 129
Dodds, R. : 61, 129
Dominion Skyways : 65
Dorval : 118, 121
Downsview : 29
Drury, G.C. "Chip" : 66, 87, 132
Drury, Peg. See Graham, Peggy
Drury, Victor M. : 25, 87
Drury, W.H.E. "Bill" : 41, 72, 111
Dunnville : 51

E

Edmonton : 89
Elementary Flying School, No. 2 : 109
Elliot Air Services : 24
"Eskimo" suit : 68

F

Fairchild Corporation : 27
Farnborough Air Show : 127
Fort William : 88
Fort William Municipal Airport : 109
Franquelin : 59

G

Garrat, P.C. : 129
George, Ronald F. : 132
German Officers : 80
Glassco, Anne : 31
Glassco, Douglas "Dougie" : 31, 33
Glassco, Gwen : 31, 126
Glassco, Margie : 31
Godbout : 60
Goldhar, Harry : 60-66
Gouzenko, Igor : 124
Graham, Peggy : 41, 44
Graham, Stuart : 41, 72, 75
Grayling, Michigan : 94
Greensville : 98
Gregor, Michael : 92
Guthrie, Tyrone : 17

H

"Hada County" : 90
Hamilton : 23, 117
Hamilton Airport : 23, 49
Hamilton Spectator : 60-66
Harrington Harbour : 75
Haswell, Stan : 126
Hatton, Bill : 3, 98
Hatton, Gwen : 53, 74, 97. See Glassco, Gwen
Hatton, Ian Malcolm : 109, 127, 130
Hatton, Joyce : 43, 59, 70, 126, 128
Hatton, Suzanne Josephine : 72
"Have a Banana" : 60-66
Havre St. Pierre : 46, 60, 71, 75, 81
Henderson, Anne : 43, 44, 55. See Glassco, Anne
Henderson, Charles : 33, 44
Hobbs, Basil W. : 129
Hornell, David : 117
Howe, C.D. : 77
Hundred Per Cent Hatton : 54

I

Imrie, Dave : 75, 79
Ingram, A.F. "Peggy" : 22, 31, 132
Ingram, Howard C. : 61
Instrument Flying Course. : 74
International Airways : 23, 24
Interprovincial Airways : 25
Irvine, W.H. "Bill" : 31, 46, 61, 119, 132

J

J.V Elliot Limited : 24
Johannesson Flying Service : 74
Joseph Brant Memorial Hospital : 130

K

Katz. Dr. : 90
King, Mackenzie : 87
Kingston : 23
Knob Lake : 119, 120
Korea : 124

L

Le Club LeMoyne : 42
Leigh, Z.L. "Lewie" : 74, 77
Lethbridge : 89
liquor permits : 108
Liskeard : 3
Loadmaster : 119
Loudon, T.R. : 129
Lymburner, Red : 75, 99
Lynes, Glen : 127

M

MacBrien, J.H. : 24
MacDonald, Sandy : 129
MacGill, Elizabeth : 92, 100, 101, 106, 112
Madore, Gary : 107
Mahon, Tom : 82
Malton : 89
Maritime Mail : 35
Martin, Bernard : 31, 37, 41, 44, 63, 133
McConachie, Grant : 89
McCurdy, John : 129
McEwen, C.M. "Black Mike" : 63, 129
McGregor, G.R. : 129
McKee Trophy : 85
McKee, J.Dalzeil : 85
McLean, Harry : 129

McNab, Ernie : 20
Moncton : 26, 38
Montreal : 23
Mooney, Major Sid : 122
Moose River : 83
Mulock, Redford H. "Red" : 26, 66, 87, 133

N

Natashquan : 75
National Aviation Museum : 79, 84, 111, 116, 117, 118
night flying : 47
North American Air Defence : 61
North Shore mail : 57
Norway, Nevile Shute : 40
nose hangar : 71

O

Old Holmstead Hotel : 70
Orenda engines : 125
Orillia : 84
Orrell, J.H. : 100
Oskelaneo : 68
Ostrander, Robert : 125
Ottawa : 89
Outardes Falls : 59

P

Packard Merlin 28 engine : 105
Palaisey, Beryl : 81
Pangborn, Clyde Edward : 115
parachutes : 51
Parker, Al : 39
Parkinson, J.D. : 25
Passchendaele : 3
Patrault, Emile : 57, 69, 74, 81, 130
Patricia Airways : 25
Pembina, North Dakota : 47
Pentecost : 59
Pettit, Anna : 55
Philately : 23
pickled onions : 110
Pike, Chris : 126
Plymouth : 3
poison gas : 4
Porquis Junction : 89
Port Harrison : 68

Port Menier : 60, 75

Q

Quebec Airways : 66
Quebec City : 59, 69

R

R-100 : 40
R101 : 40
RCAF 6 Bomber Group, : 63-66
RCAF, #1 Squadron : 21
Regina : 89
Reynolds, Arthur Edward : 22
Richardson, J.R. : 65, 66
Richmond, Richard : 120
Rimouski : 46, 72, 75, 79
RMS Duchess of Atholl : 45
RMS Duchess of Bedford : 45, 46
RMS Empress of Australia : 46
RMS Empress of Britain : 46
Robertson, J.R. : 133
Rockcliffe : 121
Rolls Royce Merlin engine : 97
Rose Lake : 68
Ross, G.M. : 61-66
Royal Air Force
    148 Squadron : 22
    242 Squadron : 107
    5 Flying Training School : 9, 12
    502 Squadron, : 15
    601 Squadron : 102
    7 (Bomber) Squadron : 14
    99 (Bomber) Squadron : 14
    Junior Commissioned Ranks : 12
    RAF Hospital Halton : 10
Royal Air Force Club : 98
Royal Canadian Air Force : 19, 46, 87, 104
Royal Flying Corps : 10, 19
Royal Mail : 35
Royal Military College : 20
Royal Naval Air Service : 10
Royal Norwegian Air Force : 93
Russell, J.J."Joe" : 104, 106

S

Sailly-sur-Lys Military Cemetery : 107
Sanderson, Jack : 129
Sanderson, Jack : 100
Saskatoon : 89
Saulsby, E.J. : 112
Saunders, Ken : 46
Schneider, A. : 46, 133
Seboies : 38
Semple, Glad : 31
Semple, Murray : 31, 66, 88, 118
Senneterre : 68, 84
Sept Isles : 60
Seymour, W.A. : 129
Shaylor, Fred : 25
Shelter Bay : 60, 67
Shuttleworth aircraft collection : 111
Sifton Lake : 68
Silver Dart : 129
Sioux Lookout : 89
Slemon, Roy : 61-66
Smith, H.C.W. "Deacon" : 133
Soulsby, E.J. : 90
Soviet Union : 124
Spadbrow, George R. : 100
Spanish Civil War : 89
Spanish G-23s : 91
St Hubert : 35, 89
St. Catherines : 42
St. Hubert : 30, 40
St. Laurent Hotel : 79
St. Lawrence River : 26
St. Louis Airport : 59
St. Louis Hotel : 59
Stationmaster Signals : 37
Stevenson Field : 79
STOL aircraft : 128
Straith, W.A. "Bill" : 78

T

Taylor, John Philip : 107
test pilot : 99
Toronto : 23, 47
Town, Jimmie : 100
Trans Canada Airlines : 77
Trinity Bay : 59
Troup, Peter : 65-66

V

Vachon, Romeo : 31, 65-66, 75, 79, 85, 134
Vickers Syndicate : 25
Victory Aircraft : 106, 125

W

Wakeman, George G. "Baldy" : 61, 91, 129
Wallace, Barnes : 40
Wallace, O.C.S. : 23, 129, 134
Warren, Bruce : 125
Waterton, Bill : 125
Weiben, Orville J. : 112
Western Canada Airways : 25
Wheeler, William J. : 93
Wingate, Alan G. : 129
Winnipeg : 26, 47, 79
Winona : 31, 123
Wogaming : 89
Woollett, Walter "Babe" : 31, 39, 42, 46, 47, 60, 61, 65, 68, 79, 111, 119
Wray, Lawrence E. : 92
Wright Field : 121
Wright- Patterson Air Force Base : 121

Y

Ypres : 2
Yukon Southern Airways : 89

Z

Zurakowski, Jan : 127, 128

The Author

James Glassco Henderson

Jim Henderson was born in July, 1929 in Burlington, Ontario, too late to enjoy the affluence of the Roaring Twenties but in plenty of time to learn about the Great Depression from his stockbroker-turned-chicken farmer father. His adolescence was spent in Brantford, Ontario where he joined the Militia. A Reserve Army commission while still in school led, after employment as a broadcaster at CKPC in Brantford, to full time military service with the Regular Army.

Early in 1950 he became editor of the Stoney Creek News, near Hamilton, but in the autumn of 1950 the far distant trumpet prevailed and he joined the Royal Canadian Horse Artillery bound for Korea. In Korea he was granted a regular commission.

During his military career he served in various artillery, staff and United Nations appointments. He commanded 2nd Surface to Surface Missile Battery, Royal Canadian Artillery and 2nd Regiment Royal Canadian Horse Artillery. He is a graduate of the British Army Staff College, Camberley, Surrey and the United States Armed Forces Staff College, Norfolk, Virginia. He also served on the faculty of the Canadian Forces Command and Staff College, Toronto.

On retiring from the Canadian Forces in 1978, he joined the news staff at CHAY FM radio in Barrie, Ontario eventually becoming the station's News Director and Operations Manager.

From 1994 to 1999 he produced a quarterly publication, Military Digest, which was circulated by subscription. He has contributed regularly to two military publications, and is a member of the Canadian Institute of Strategic Studies and the Canadian Aviation Historical Society.

This is his second book to be published by Trafford. His first, *The Nuking of Happy Valley*" is a collection of amusing anecdotes from his military career.

ISBN 141203897-9